It All Depends

It All Depends

*A Casebook for Prospective Teachers of
Students Who Are Deaf and Hard of Hearing*

SECOND EDITION

Carl B. Williams

Butte Publications, Inc.
Hillsboro, Oregon USA

It All Depends

A Casebook for Prospective Teachers of Students Who Are Deaf and Hard of Hearing

SECOND EDITION

© 2015 Butte Publications, Inc.

All rights reserved. No part of this publication may be reproduced or transmitted in any form or by any means, electronic or mechanical, including photocopy, recording, or any retrieval system, without permission in writing from the publisher.

Editor: Ellen Todras
Design: Anita Jones, Another Jones Graphics

Butte Publications, Inc.
P.O. Box 1328
Hillsboro, Oregon 97123-1328
U.S.A.
www.buttepublications.com

ISBN: 978-1-939349-09-5

Table of Contents

ACKNOWLEDGMENTS vii

PREFACE ix

PART 1 COMMUNICATION ISSUES 1
    Case 1   Listen Up 3
    Case 2   All Eyes on Me 7
    Case 3   Is That Possible? 11
    Case 4   Overwhelming Joy 15
    Case 5   Active Voice 19

PART 2 LITERACY INSTRUCTION 23
    Case 6   Exercises in Futility 25
    Case 7   First Things First 31
    Case 8   Get It In Writing 37
    Case 9   Poetic License 41
    Case 10 Put to the Test 45

PART 3 CONTENT INSTRUCTION 49
    Case 11 Cultural Literacy 51
    Case 12 A Textbook Example 57
    Case 13 A Word to the Wise 61
    Case 14 Bad Science 65
    Case 15 You Do the Math 69

PART 4 LEARNER DIFFERENCES 73
    Case 16 Include Me In 75
    Case 17 Things Just Don't Add Up 81
    Case 18 Disorderly Conduct 85
    Case 19 Spoiled for Choice 91
    Case 20 Same Difference 95

PART 5 EDUCATIONAL PLANNING 99

    Case 21 A Valuable Lesson 101
    Case 22 The Ultimate Goal 107
    Case 23 A Smooth Transition...111
    Case 24 Proposed Merger..117
    Case 25 From Finish to Start 121

APPENDIX
    Sample Rubrics for Assessing Students' Responses
    to Cases 125

REFERENCES & RELATED READINGS 129

GLOSSARY..133

Acknowledgments

Above all, I owe a huge debt of gratitude to Matt Brink, who said "yes" to me one more time and who believed from the start that a Deaf Education casebook would be a resource worthy of publication.

I also wish to thank Ellen Todras for her editorial contributions in the form of helpful questions and suggestions that guided my revisions.

My appreciation also extends to Anita Jones, whose graphic design expertise yielded a polished final product.

I am especially grateful to the many readers whose interest motivated them to purchase the first edition of *It All Depends*.

A special thank you goes to teacher educators who determined that *It All Depends* was a useful addition to their college and university courses.

I also thank my former students, who now have their own classroom stories and are amenable to sharing some of the more compelling ones with me.

Finally, I want to acknowledge the administration at Flagler College for granting me a sabbatical, which allowed me the reflective time to complete this project.

Preface

It All Depends: A Casebook for Prospective Teachers of Students Who Are Deaf and Hard of Hearing is a text supplement for use in foundations and methods courses in Deaf Education. It will be useful in helping preservice teachers make important connections between knowledge and application of educational concepts and principles. Accordingly, it is assumed that teacher candidates have had some exposure to issues that impact the education of deaf and hard of hearing students, such as IEPs, literacy instruction, Deaf culture, assessment, multiple disabilities, communication methods, standards-based education, transition, and classroom management.

The approach taken in this casebook is consistent with trends in teacher education that are intended to promote critical thinking, inquiry, and reflection regarding pedagogical situations within a specific educational context. Preservice teachers are able to synthesize information from their professors, textbooks, field experiences, and common sense to inform decisions about high-probability strategies that might be effective in the scenarios presented in the cases. Discussing cases and real solutions to real problems encountered in real classrooms places prospective teachers of deaf and hard of hearing students in an authentic teacher role: continuously reflecting on pedagogical decisions to enhance student achievement. Moreover, not only are they expected to state *what* they would do but also *why*.

This casebook consists of five chapters with five case studies in each chapter. The cases reflect issues involved in teaching students who are deaf and cover a variety of situations categorized into five broad areas: communication issues, literacy instruction, content instruction, learner differences, and educational planning. As such, they represent situations relevant to prospective teachers in grades K–12. Although grade levels are stated in each case, the circumstances

It All Depends

can be generalized to any student in any grade experiencing the problem under study. Also, a single case will usually allow for the consideration and discussion of multiple issues, which may lend themselves to multiple perspectives and resolutions.

The specific scenarios are based on the author's 38 years in the field of Deaf Education. They are drawn from direct experiences (as a classroom teacher), observations of inservice teachers (as a consultant and curriculum specialist), and observations of preservice teachers (as a teacher educator). The teacher in each scenario is identified as a beginning teacher for two reasons. First, this status reflects the first professional roles that preservice teachers will assume in the field of education. Second, this stage of development allows for the exploration of a wider number of issues determined to be problematic based on the presumption that it is the teacher's first encounter with them. In some shape or form, these cases have been used over the years with my students, who have commented favorably that the cases were an effective catalyst for compelling them to synthesize knowledge they have acquired from various courses and field experiences in their program of study.

Each case contains the following: (1) a scenario with one or more educational issues that are problematic, (2) reflection questions that encourage students to consider a variety of workable solutions by approaching problems with information acquired in their courses and field experiences, and (3) extension activities that will allow students to broaden and refine their knowledge and skills relative to the issues embedded within the cases under study. The reflection questions may be discussed in class or answered in writing, or a combination of both expressive processes may be used. The questions and activities are, by no means, exhaustive. Indeed, instructors and students are encouraged to generate additional questions and pursue additional activities related to the cases under study.

While there are specific pedagogical principles that derive from each case, the intent is not to be prescriptive regarding particular strategies, techniques, and activities that might be used to address problematic issues. For example, if a case were to suggest that students' writing was unfocused and disorganized because the teacher failed to allow time during which students could have received assistance and guidance with selecting and organizing their ideas, there are many different prewriting strategies that could be suggested. Some of these strategies are drawing, outlining, brainstorming, using graphic organizers, mapping, listing, cubing, and role playing. All of these might be considered appropriate ways to address the problem in this case. This approach reflects the belief that good teachers possess a repertoire of strategies to implement effective instruction.

Some cases might provide what may be viewed as limited information for consideration. As Kauffman and Landrum (2009) note, rarely do cases present the totality of information desired by readers. However, they rightfully point out that even in real-life situations, educational professionals often find it necessary to draw tentative conclusions and make decisions without the benefit of all the information they might wish to have. In these instances, readers are encouraged to (1) analyze the scenarios based on the details in the cases and (2) make any necessary contextual inferences that are reasonable and relevant.

Case studies have become increasingly valued as a beneficial way to have preservice teachers critically analyze situations in which they might find themselves as interns and future teachers. Like practicing teachers, they are expected to formulate a strategic plan of action after evaluating the facts, weighing the pros and cons of possible solutions, and selecting choices most likely to produce the maximum benefit and the least detriment. Effective teachers choose what they have determined to be the most meritorious solution and mitigate, to the extent possible, any foreseeable disadvantages. This process is reflected in the main title of this casebook, *It All Depends*, which conveys the fact that teaching does not occur in a vacuum. In fact, one of the criticisms of teacher education programs is that students enrolled in them often learn concepts and theories, but they cannot evaluate them and apply them in the context of real-life instances.

The title is resonant because often my undergraduate students will tell me, sportively, that the statement "It all depends" is my recurrent response to many of their questions. Actually, I find this observation a complimentary one because, as a teacher educator, I am hopefully modeling the reality that there are no one-size-fits-all solutions to specific educational problems experienced by specific students.

Even when I do inservice activities for practicing teachers, I am sometimes asked questions similar to those asked by my college students. Those practicing teachers receive the same answer with which I respond to my students. For example, during the course of a language arts inservice session at an elementary school, a teacher asked me, "What's the best strategy for teaching spelling?" My response? "It all depends." In this case—on the misspelled words. Since her classroom was nearby, I requested that she bring me a student's most recent spelling quiz. When she returned and handed me the paper, I wrote the four misspelled words on a transparency and placed it on the overhead projector. The transparency contained these misspelled words: *did'ent, somtime, feild,* and *forteen.*

I explained that in this case, rather than a single best strategy, I would use three different approaches: teaching a mini-lesson on forming contractions (for *didn't*), teaching the "i" before "e" rule (for *field*), and teaching a mini-lesson on compound words (for *sometime* and *fourteen*). The student's quiz was powerful in helping me to make my overarching point. Strategies have the potential to be "best" or "effective" only to the extent that they match the context of specific learning needs.

The Council for Exceptional Children's (CEC) standards for beginning teachers of students who are deaf and hard of hearing include Skill DH1S1: *apply theories, philosophies, and models of practice to the education of individuals who are deaf or hard of hearing.* This casebook can be used to support texts and instruction in foundations courses, methods courses, and student teaching seminars to provide Deaf Education majors with opportunities to practice this skill. To this end, teacher educators are encouraged to use this book in a nonlinear manner, selecting those cases pertinent to the Deaf Education courses and competencies they teach.

PREFACE

NEW TO THIS EDITION

In preparing this second edition, I had in mind a single goal: to expand and to upgrade the previous work. Although the basic organization of the casebook remains the same, two new cases have been added in each of the five chapters. Care was taken to avoid simply replicating the primary issues from the cases presented in the first edition and to include other relevant issues such as self-advocacy, additional disabilities, differentiated instruction, alternative achievement standards, consulting with general education teachers, and working with challenging parents.

Also, a glossary has been included to define or explain over 50 key terms and concepts used in the various cases. Furthermore, rubrics for evaluating student responses to reflective questions have been included in an appendix. In fact, two sample rubrics are provided: one for an evaluation of individual questions; the other, for an evaluation of the processes involved in reflecting on the cases. Instructors may have a preference for one or the other. Alternatively, they may choose to develop a different scoring guide that better meets their course assessment needs. Finally, there are updated and new references, which more than double the number of entries in the bibliography that concluded the first edition.

I wrote the first edition after obtaining copies of four special education casebooks, intending to extract the ones related to deafness for use with my students. Much to my surprise, there was not a single case that met this criterion. It was as if deafness did not exist as a special education disability category. Shortly thereafter, I recalled a Toni Morrison quotation: "If there's a book that you want to read, but it hasn't been written yet, then you must write it." In 2006, I followed Ms. Morrison's suggestion, and the first edition of *It All Depends* was published as a result. In this new edition, if the enhancements made have resulted in an even more valuable resource that teacher educators can use to supplement traditional classroom instruction, the process of updating it will have been completely worthwhile.

Part 1:
Communication Issues

Case 1: Listen Up

Jacob Palmer is a first-year teacher in a day school for deaf students. His class consists of six first-grade students, ages five and six, with hearing losses ranging between 35 and 70 dB. Because his students have mild or moderate losses, he is especially concerned about monitoring their hearing aid use.

One day recently, after he made sure the FM batteries were charged, Jacob placed the transmitter in his pocket and clipped the microphone to the lapel of his shirt. Then he asked his students to raise their hands if their hearing aids were on. He follows this routine every morning, because he knows the importance of amplification for helping his students develop and enhance their speech skills.

The first lesson of the day was a social skills activity: helping others. On the interactive whiteboard, Jacob had displayed the words "Helping Others." He pointed at the words and told the students they would be learning different ways to help other people, and that people feel good when they do nice things for other people. He then directed them to watch the board. He accessed the videotape feature, and the clip started. It portrayed a man struggling as he carried four books, one of which eventually fell to the floor. A young girl saw the situation and began walking toward the man. At this juncture, Jacob stopped the videotape and asked the students what they thought the little girl was going to do.

Kayla raised her hand and, rather than offering a response as Jacob had expected, said that her hearing aid wasn't making his voice loud enough. He looked to make sure the aid was in the "on" position and that the volume was turned up. He shrugged his shoulders and said he would contact the audiologist later to try to figure out the problem. Since Kayla had indicated she could hear his voice, albeit at a low volume, he instructed her to continue to wear the hearing aid for the rest of the day. Jacob proceeded with the lesson by having the

It All Depends

students pair off, pretend they were in one of three situations he provided, and act out what they would do. He provided feedback and concluded with ways people help others in school and at home.

After the social skills lesson was completed, the class did a mathematics activity: skip counting by twos. After Jacob explained the process, students were directed to skip count until they reached the number 20, as he pointed to the appropriate numbers on a number line. When the group reached the number 10, Carlos's hearing aid began to whistle. Jacob halted the group's recitation and checked the aid. He knew to lower the volume if it was set too high. The volume setting was fine. He also knew that feedback could result from an improperly inserted earmold, so he pressed the earmold snugly into Carlos's ear. Unfortunately, the feedback persisted. Jacob asked Carlos to remove the hearing aid, because the whistling would be bothersome to everyone. He explained to Carlos that he would contact the district's audiologist shortly and have her take a look at the hearing aid to determine the problem.

When Jacob's instructional aide came to take his students to physical education class during his planning time, he called the audiologist and explained the problems with the two hearing aids and how he had tried to resolve them, to no avail. The audiologist said that she had a number of other school visits to make, but she would stop by at 3:00. She added that after examining the hearing aids, she would like to talk with Jacob for about 30 minutes. Since the students left at 2:30 and his workday did not officially end until 3:30, he indicated that this arrangement was fine with him.

After finishing the conversation, Jacob reflected on the tone of the audiologist's response to his request for assistance. She seemed polite enough. However, although she didn't say so directly, she seemed to suggest that maybe he hadn't done all he could have done regarding the hearing aid problems his students experienced. Her reaction was surprising, he thought, because he felt he had done a decent job of trying to troubleshoot the problems and match solutions with symptoms.

He decided to put his uneasiness on the back burner for the moment. Right now, he needed to set up a science experiment for his

Case 1: LISTEN UP

students, who would be returning shortly. The situation with the audiologist would be clarified later in the day.

QUESTIONS FOR REFLECTION

1. What are the key issues presented in this case?
2. What are possible reasons that Kayla might have perceived low volume other than those Jacob Palmer checked?
3. What are possible reasons for the feedback from Carlos's hearing aid other than those Jacob Palmer checked?
4. At what age do you think the responsibility for hearing aid checks should shift from teacher to student? Think about the grade level you plan or would like to teach. What responsibilities for hearing aid maintenance would you reasonably expect students in this grade to assume?
5. What are some ways teachers can troubleshoot hearing aid problems aurally?
6. What are some ways that hearing and deaf teachers can troubleshoot hearing aid problems visually?

EXTENSION ACTIVITIES

1. Contact an audiologist or a hearing aid technician. Ask him or her what types of hearing aid problems would be reasonable to expect classroom teachers to take care of.
2. Contact several teachers of the deaf who teach students K–12. What types of hearing aid troubleshooting have their students demonstrated they can handle in elementary school, middle school, and high school?
3. Consult your hearing science text and several hearing aid websites. Develop your own troubleshooting matrix that synthesizes information from these sources. Include in the matrix a column for "Common Hearing Aid Problems" and a corresponding column for each problem called "Solutions to Try."

Case 2: All Eyes on Me

Brianna Adams felt prepared to teach ninth-grade social studies in a self-contained classroom located in a public high school because she had done her internship in a similar setting with the same age level. The benchmark she planned to teach was the following: "Discuss the effects of the Industrial Revolution." Brianna had graduated with a dual major: social science and Deaf Education. The Industrial Revolution was one of her favorite historical topics, and she looked forward to sharing this information with her eight students. They all had severe to profound hearing losses and used Total Communication. Two of the students had received cochlear implants three years ago and had been slowly developing speech skills, which they used along with signs.

Brianna stood at the opening of the horseshoe configuration into which she had arranged the students' desks. She briskly waved both hands in the "R" handshape and said that she was ready to begin the day's lesson. She explained that they would be learning about inventions that grew out of advances that occurred during a time period called the Industrial Revolution. Then, she proceeded with the introduction to the lesson. She began by stating the names of the two men, Louis-Auguste Blanqui and Fredrich Engels, credited with introducing the term *Industrial Revolution*. Next, she explained that the dates for the period are not precise, but that historians generally agree upon the time span 1760–1830.

About five minutes into her lesson introduction, just when she was going to build on the time element and point out that it spanned the reigns of British kings George III and William IV, Brianna noticed that Jasmine had turned slightly and was signing a series of comments unrelated to the lesson to a classmate, Doug. Doug was trying to stifle a laugh. Although Brianna didn't catch the whole exchange, it seemed to be about something amusing that happened when Jasmine's family

It All Depends

had gone to the movies the previous night. Brianna directed a disapproving glance in their direction. This strategy worked for a minute or so, but soon the two students were engaging in another side conversation. To make matters worse, as Brianna continued explaining how the Industrial Revolution affects us today, two other students, Alvin and Josh, began conversing in sign about the lunch menu and what they hoped would be served.

In the time she tried to prepare the class with necessary background information on the Industrial Revolution, Brianna had to stop a total of eight times to redirect students' attention to her. The disruptions and interventions had absorbed so much time that when she was ready to move to the next phase of the lesson, a student did the time-out gesture and pointed to the clock. Time had indeed flown by, but Brianna wasn't having any fun. With an audible and visible sigh, she dismissed her students and told them they would continue the lesson the following day. As he was leaving, Josh turned and asked if they were going to learn about different inventors. She managed a weak smile and indicated that they would learn about them later.

Brianna sat at her desk, her expression weary, and wondered what went wrong. A sense of frustration roiled inside of her, because she was so proud of this lesson. The Industrial Revolution and inventors/inventions were separate benchmarks in the social studies curriculum. She figured she could cover both benchmarks in a single lesson, because inventions were a positive byproduct of the Industrial Revolution. Being able to kill two birds with one stone would greatly help her teach all of the required benchmarks by the end of the academic year.

Finally, she did some serious soul-searching. Maybe the lesson introduction had dragged on too long, she conceded, but the knowledge she was trying to impart was essential to the students' understanding of subsequent information that would be presented in the unit. How could she justify making short shrift of the initial phase of the lesson? If the students had only persevered, she would have passed out some pictures of inventors that they would try to match with the inventions. In addition to the conventional inventions presented in the textbook, she had included inventions that might resonate more with

Case 2: ALL EYES ON ME

the students, such as potato chips, blue jeans, and the TTY. She was certain the activity would be both enlightening and enjoyable.

She also wondered if she had spent too much time stopping the lesson and demanding students' attention. However, she felt her interventions were warranted, remembering something from an educational psychology book about paying attention being the first step in learning. In the remaining moments before the next class was to begin, she also thought briefly about the U-shaped seating. Sure, it allowed students to see her and each other easily. Then again, visual access to each other seemed to be part of the problem she had experienced earlier. Perhaps she could experiment with another seating arrangement. In the self-contained classrooms she had visited during her field experiences, though, students were seated in a horseshoe formation. And their teachers were more experienced than she.

Still disillusioned, she heard the door open, alerting her that a new class period was about to begin. As she was shifting gears mentally, she was pleased that she had taken time for reflection, a process she had learned in her college courses was critically important for teachers. Yes, she had reflected on the attention problem, but her reflection seemed to result in no clear-cut answers, only more questions. At any rate, she resolved to think about her instructional dilemma some more this evening, taking heart as she suddenly recalled Scarlett O'Hara's optimistic perspective in *Gone with the Wind*: "After all, tomorrow is another day!"

QUESTIONS FOR REFLECTION

1. What are the key issues presented in this case?
2. Obviously, there is a correlation between good instruction and good classroom management. With that perspective as an assumption, do you think the situation Brianna encountered was *primarily* an instructional issue or a classroom management issue? Explain the rationale for your answer.
3. Base your answer to this question on your response to the previous question.

It All Depends

- If you felt the situation in the case was primarily an instructional issue, what are some strategies Brianna could have used to deliver instruction more effectively?
- If you felt the situation in the case was primarily a classroom management issue, what are some strategies Brianna could have used to minimize the disruptions that occurred during the lesson?

Extension Activities

1. Two theories in which *attention* is a critical component are Information Processing Theory and Social Cognitive Theory (also called Social Learning Theory). Consult an educational psychology textbook or access the Internet, and explain the role of *attention* in both of these theories.
2. Contact teachers of the deaf who teach at different grade levels. List strategies teachers use to gain and maintain the attention of students in elementary school, in middle school, and in high school.

CASE 3: IS THAT POSSIBLE?

Dustin Corley is a congenitally deaf 10-year-old boy. His parents are both deaf and have communicated with him using American Sign Language (ASL) since his birth. Speech and auditory skills are not his strengths, but he does wear a hearing aid and will attempt to use his speech in the cafeteria, at recess, or at other times when his educational interpreter, Vivian Candelas, is not close by. These communication attempts are usually successful for two reasons. First, they are limited to words for which there is an obvious visual reference. Second, they are limited to concepts for which there are commonly understood gestures, which Dustin and his peers use to support comprehension during their interactions.

Although Dustin's English skills are good and he enjoys reading, his main passion is mathematics. He has a facility with numbers, and he mastered basic arithmetic skills quickly. His grades in math are commendable. When math lessons are novel and challenging, he becomes particularly excited. This was the case when his teacher, Ms. Santaloci, displayed a deck of cards and some colored cubes on the desk in front of the classroom.

Dustin looked momentarily at the manipulatives and then to the interpreter, who was beginning to sign the teacher's introduction and lesson objective. Ms. Santaloci said, "Today you are going to determine if an event is <u>certain</u>, <u>probable</u>, or <u>impossible</u>. This is one of the state-required mathematics skills for fourth graders, so you need to pay careful attention."

Indeed, Dustin attended closely as Ms. Santaloci's introduction was conveyed by Vivian Candelas, who was conspicuously pondering her repertoire of options for conveying the objective's key concepts: certain, probable, and impossible. She decided to use the sign "true" for <u>certain</u>, the sign "maybe" for <u>probable</u>, and the sign "can't" for <u>impossible</u>.

It All Depends

    Ms. Santoloci placed three red cubes and a single blue cube in a box and asked, "What is the probability of reaching in and pulling a blue cube from the box?" Dustin eagerly raised his hand and signed, "True." The interpreter voiced, "Certain." The teacher replied, "No, that's not correct, Dustin," and proceeded to call on another student, who provided the correct response, "Probable." Dustin displayed an expression of disbelief. He was profoundly perplexed. It seemed as if there could be two answers to the question. He thought that one could "maybe" pull out a blue cube, but it was also "true" that one could remove a blue cube.

    Ms. Santoloci asked, "What is the probability of removing a yellow cube?" Dustin decided to test his knowledge once more. When called on, he signed, "Can't." The interpreter voiced, "Impossible." The teacher smiled and praised Dustin for his correct answer. He felt good, and his previous state of confusion dissipated. Ms. Santoloci presented some other examples and eventually said, "Class, this is my final example," holding up a deck of cards and then spreading them on the table. She picked up one card and asked, "What is the probability that I have a king in my hand?" Dustin raised his hand and decided to test his theory of two right answers. When recognized, he signed, "True or Maybe." The interpreter voiced, "Certain or Probable." Ms. Santaloci said, "Dustin, there's only one correct answer. I'm not sure you completely understand the concept yet."

    Dustin was deflated and momentarily closed his eyes. When he did so, his thoughts transported him back to the beginning of the lesson. He recalled the furrowed brows of the interpreter when Ms. Santoloci started her explanation. Perhaps Vivian Candelas had misunderstood the teacher and signed the information incorrectly. Dustin knew that the itinerant teacher, Mrs. Collins, would be at his school tomorrow. He would make an appointment to see her and let her know that he wanted a different interpreter.

Case 3: IS THAT POSSIBLE?

QUESTIONS FOR REFLECTION

1. What are the key issues presented in this case?
2. What responsibility does the educational interpreter bear regarding Dustin's consternation and dismay?
3. What responsibility does the teacher bear regarding Dustin's consternation and dismay?
4. What are some ways that the situation with Dustin could have been avoided and his comprehension enhanced?
5. Do you think that Dustin's proposed course of action identified at the end of the case has merit? Why or why not?

EXTENSION ACTIVITIES

1. Contact several Exceptional Student Education (ESE) Directors in different districts or states and find out the answers to the following questions: What kinds of monitoring and evaluation procedures are in place for educational interpreters? Who does the monitoring? How frequently is the monitoring done? What kind of training is provided to regular education teachers to help them work effectively with interpreters? Are there IEP goals designed to help deaf students work effectively with interpreters?
2. Access the Registry of Interpreters for the Deaf website: www.rid.org/eduterp.html. Select several states of interest, and identify their minimum training and certification standards for educational sign language interpreters.

Case 4: Overwhelming Joy

Anya Cazden could barely contain her jubilation as she waited for her six first graders to arrive. When she was studying Deaf Education in college, people would ask her the age group she wanted to teach. Although her peers would often say they did not know or that it made no difference, for Anya, the answer was easy. She had always had her heart set on teaching first grade. Throughout high school, she had babysat for a variety of age levels, but she seemed to have a particular affinity for the children just starting their formal schooling. These children would spiritedly share their schoolwork and delighted in detailing what they had learned in school that day. And the myriad questions they asked about everything under the sun created an atmosphere of inquiry and curiosity that she wanted to cultivate—and participate in!—on a daily basis.

Anya would be the first to acknowledge that serious work was necessary to lay some important learning foundations for first graders, with language development being one of the most important. She looked forward to working in this oral program, located in a tight-knit community, where most of the students' homes were not far from the school itself. She had interned in a similar program and, as a result, felt comfortable in this setting in which her students, all of whom wore hearing aids or had cochlear implants, had parents who expected them to listen to the greatest extent possible and produce intelligible speech. She realized that she would need to focus on communication at two levels. First, she needed to become familiar with her students' auditory devices and listening profiles to ensure that aural-oral communication was maximized. Second, she needed to focus relentlessly on language development. The students' kindergarten teacher had collected language samples from each child and included her report in their files, which Anya had gone over with a fine-tooth comb. IEP goals had been developed to

It All Depends

address deficiencies, and Anya was determined to make these goals a focal point of her curricular programming.

In an effort to do some advance work, Anya decided to go online to view the state curriculum standards to get a sense of how she might align the IEP goals with these learning outcomes. Anxiety began to wash over her as she perceived the rigor of the academic expectations for first graders. She sampled the mathematics and English language arts standards (her state was using the Common Core):

- *Given a two-digit number, mentally find 10 more or 10 less than the number, without having to count; explain the reasoning used.*
- *Produce and expand complete simple and compound declarative, interrogative, imperative, and exclamatory sentences in response to prompts.*

Next, she sampled the state standards in science and social studies.

- *Compare and contrast physical properties and composition of objects.*
- *Identify people and events observed in national celebrations and holidays.*

Anya now found herself in complete panic mode as the full weight of her teaching responsibilities pressed down on her. In 180 days, she was expected to attend to the following areas: language development, listening skills, speech facilitation, general curriculum standards, and IEP goals. *And what am I going to do with my extra time?* she thought wryly, trying to cheer herself up. Realistically, she reminded herself that even though she was alone in the classroom, she was not alone in the educational enterprise. She was part of a professional team and, at every available opportunity, she would be seeking the assistance of her colleagues and her students' parents.

Even so, she knew her responsibilities would require a considerable investment of time. However, when her reflection was interrupted by the lively entrance of six bundles of energy wearing smiling faces and electronic devices, she allowed herself one additional thought. The investment of time, regardless of how prodigious it turned out to be, would be more than worthwhile.

Case 4: OVERWHELMING JOY

Questions for Reflection

1. What are the key issues presented in the case?
2. How can teachers of the deaf integrate speech and auditory development goals with English language arts standards? Provide one specific example.
3. How can teachers integrate English language arts standards with content-area standards in math, science, and social studies? Provide one specific example for each subject.
4. Identify two colleagues from whom Anya might solicit assistance. How might they be able to help her optimize the listening environment and learning experiences for her students?

Extension Activities

1. Identify four specific models for integrating curriculum within a single discipline and across multiple disciplines.
2. Specify two speech articulation goals and two auditory processing goals that might be used to support the aural-oral development of deaf and hard of hearing students.
3. Two common ways of working with other professionals in school settings involve *consultation* and *collaboration*. Do some research on the two models, and explain the interactions involved in each process that will increase the likelihood of positive working relationships and favorable learning outcomes for students.

Case 5: Active Voice

When first-year teacher Arden Sandoval left the office of her supervisor, Director of Itinerant Services Brielle Hollander, she drove to a consultation at one of the schools she served in a medium-sized school district in the Northeast. As she sat in the library of the school, waiting to talk about captioned programming with the media specialist, Arden reflected on her meeting with Ms. Hollander, who explained that the district had decided to encourage greater participation by all students with disabilities in their IEP conferences beginning the following school year. The initial focus would be on secondary students. Arden was directed to prepare one student to lead his or her IEP conference in the spring. Afterward, she would submit a status report, complete with benefits, challenges, and recommendations for wider student participation next fall.

The IEP initiative resonated powerfully with Arden for three reasons. First, it provided some opportunity for direct instruction. Most of the students in her caseload functioned very well in their classes, so most of her contact was with other adults. And she had to admit, she missed direct contact with students. Second, she always had a keen interest in career counseling. In fact, she was investigating online master's degree programs in guidance counseling, which would help further this desire to provide personal, educational, and vocational support to deaf and hard of hearing students. Third, the concept simply made sense. Special educators frequently emphasized the importance of students with disabilities improving their self-advocacy skills. The IEP meeting seemed to be an ideal authentic situation in which to apply them.

After a productive meeting with the media specialist, Arden exited the school and entered her mobile office, snapped her seat belt into place, and made her way to a meeting with the assistant principal/assessment coordinator of an elementary school to discuss test accommodations. While in transit, she was desperately trying to

It All Depends

come up with the name of a student to prepare for the IEP conference initiative. As she drove along, taking in the brilliant colors of the fall foliage, a name suddenly came to mind: Cooper Paxton.

Cooper Paxton, a highly intelligent young man, is a junior. He has a mild hearing loss, and his speech is sufficiently intelligible that he can be understood by his classmates, teachers, and other adults in the school environment. He has expressed a desire to attend college, and he certainly has the grades to be successful. A quality he does lack, which will be indispensable to him in college, is self-advocacy. Even though he has skills that should make interaction in a mainstream setting a relatively easy undertaking, he has contacted Arden several times since the start of school to intervene on his behalf regarding routine matters that he could have handled himself. Meeting with him on a weekly basis would provide her with an opportunity to discuss self-advocacy skills and give him regular assignments that will require that he use these skills in realistic situations.

Arden made arrangements to meet once a week with Cooper, pulling him from his Advancement Via Individual Determination (AVID) class, an elective course designed to provide students with the academic support they need to reach their fullest potential and attend college. During their first meeting, as Arden explained the increased level of participation he would assume in his spring IEP meeting, he gave her an incredulous look, and his respiration visibly quickened.

"Take a few deep breaths," Arden said reassuringly. "The process is not going to be as difficult as you might think. I wouldn't ask you to do something if I didn't believe you could do it. You know that."

Nervously, he said, "I go to my IEP meetings every year, and they seem complicated. How will I know what to do?"

Arden laughed. "Then we have something in common. This is the first IEP conference I am responsible for. So I decided we will co-lead the conference this year, and next year, perhaps you might feel confident moderating the conference, with support from me. Plus, we still have six months to figure things out and practice by role-playing our parts. I promise you: We'll be ready!"

Case 5: ACTIVE VOICE

Cooper's heart rate noticeably subsided. He let out a big sigh of relief and said, "That sounds like a good plan."

Arden added, "And it's a plan that benefits you as a young man one year away from graduation. Unlike your previous IEP meetings, instead of other people speaking for you...."

Cooper finished her statement. "I can speak for myself." He smiled faintly, as if this idea of IEP leadership was beginning to grow on him.

Arden displayed two thumbs up and said, "And that's what self-advocacy is all about." She stood and shook Cooper's hand, relieved that he appeared more confident than he had at the start of the discussion.

After he left, she opened her laptop and did an online search for self-advocacy. The first article she located indicated that there are four basic components: self-awareness, knowledge of rights, communication, and leadership. Just what she needed, Arden thought. She did not have a comprehensive plan of attack yet, but she did know one thing: Cooper's spring IEP would definitely include goals related to each of these four areas. As thoughts began to percolate about the content of these goals, she began to furiously type notes into her laptop. With immense delight, she observed her unformed ideas crystallizing, laughing heartily as she recalled the words of the A-Team's Hannibal: "I love it when a plan comes together."

QUESTIONS FOR REFLECTION

1. What are the key issues presented in the case?
2. IDEA states that students with disabilities must be included in the IEP process "whenever appropriate." Although the law is not specific about when those "appropriate times" are, what are some instances in which participation by students in their IEP conferences might be especially warranted?
3. What would be one goal that can be established for Cooper in each of the four self-advocacy domains listed below?
    - self-awareness

It All Depends

- knowledge of rights
- communication
- leadership

4. What are two specific ways that Arden can scaffold and support Cooper's participation during the course of his actual IEP conference?

EXTENSION ACTIVITIES

1. Identify five sites designed to provide tools and resources that support students with disabilities in developing self-advocacy skills.
2. Locate a self-advocacy or self-determination checklist. In one of your field experiences, select a student or a class, administer the survey, summarize the results, and share them with the teacher.
3. Identify specific strategies for assisting parents in promoting self-advocacy skills in their children who are deaf or hard of hearing.

Part 2:
Literacy Instruction

Case 6: Exercises in Futility

Krista Larson was very excited as she sat in the classroom, this time not as a preservice teacher but as a certified teacher. Having graduated from a deaf education program in another state, she was happy about returning to her home state of Nevada to begin her teaching career. She had landed her first job as a teacher of seven eighth graders in a self-contained classroom in a public middle school. Their hearing losses ranged between 80 and 90 dB, and sign language was their primary method of communication.

Krista felt comfortable with teaching the content-area subjects: mathematics, science, health, and social studies. However, she was somewhat anxious about teaching English language arts, because she had learned in her undergraduate program that reading and writing posed particular problems for deaf students, especially those with greater degrees of hearing loss. Also, logic would indicate that if her students were not having problems with literacy skills, they probably would have been mainstreamed into the regular classroom.

Krista was also aware that, as a part of the statewide testing program, students' writing proficiency would be assessed for all eighth graders. Accordingly, she felt a tremendous responsibility to enhance her students' literacy skills.

Because her language courses had spent the lion's share of time on the reading process and not the writing process, Krista was more comfortable planning for reading instruction so, during her planning period, she decided to begin with what she felt was her most challenging task: planning for writing instruction. She remembered that starting with assessment was important, and she was thankful that last year's teacher had passed on some writing samples she could review and use as the basis for establishing objectives for next week's lessons. She realized that she needed to ensure that her instructional unit also prepared students for the writing assessment.

It All Depends

She decided to access the Nevada Department of Education's website, where she found that scoring for the Eighth Grade Writing Proficiency Exam was based on four criteria: ideas, organization, voice, and conventions.

With this information in mind, Krista began to read the students' writing samples. She was pleasantly surprised that the students' ideas were sound, the organization of their writing was logical and easy to follow, and there was a strong sense of voice in the compositions. The most pressing issue was a limited control of the conventions of written English. Overall, their spelling, punctuation, and capitalization were fine, but their grammar was problematic, especially regarding use of past tense—even when there was a time element stated—and omission of prepositions in prepositional phrases. Therefore, Krista determined that these two areas would form the basis of writing instruction for the next couple of weeks.

Searching the bookshelves, Krista was delighted to find a grammar skills work text entitled *Essential English Skills*. The teacher's manual stated that the purpose of the textbook was to help students develop basic grammar and composition skills and that the interest level made it appropriate for grades 6–12. The estimated reading level, 2.0 (based on the Spache Readability Formula), was consistent with her students' reading scores, which ranged from 1.9 to 2.3. When she perused the book and found sections on past-tense verbs and prepositional phrases, she felt that she had struck pay dirt and decided to use it as the basis for her grammar lessons.

Over the course of the next two weeks, Krista used the work text as her guide, employing the explanations and exercises prescribed in the book. The first week, she concentrated on past-tense verbs. Adhering to the sequence of the book, she did the following:

- She explained that past tense shows past time.
- She explained that verbs, called regular verbs, indicate past tense by adding *d* or *ed*.
- She pointed out that irregular verbs do not and had them memorize the past forms of 30 irregular verbs.
- She had the students circle the verbs in each of 20 sentences.

Case 6: EXERCISES IN FUTILITY

- She had students write present or past to indicate the verb tense in 20 sentences.
- She had students circle the correct form of irregular past-tense verbs in 20 sentences.
- She had students write 20 sentences for 10 past-tense verbs that she provided.

The second week, she worked on prepositional phrases. Adhering to the sequence of the book, she did the following:

- She explained that prepositions connect words or groups of words.
- She gave the students a list of words commonly used as prepositions.
- She explained that a prepositional phrase included the preposition plus the noun that follows it and showed examples.
- She had students underline the prepositional phrases in 20 sentences.
- She had the students write 20 sentences, using prepositional phrases that she provided.

Krista was pleased that all of her students performed satisfactorily on all of the exercises. Moreover, they wrote some good sentences using the target structures.

The following week, after a field trip to the local newspaper, Krista decided to have her students write an account of their trip, thinking this activity would be an opportunity for them to use past-tense verbs and prepositional phrases. At the end of the school day, she sat down to read the compositions. As she did so, feelings of inadequacy and failure washed over her as she read paper after paper with almost no past-tense forms of verbs, even regular ones, and a glaring omission of prepositions to show relationships between concepts.

She crossed out the present-tense verb forms and wrote the past-tense forms above them, and she inserted carets where prepositions should be, writing the relevant prepositions above the carets. She then placed the papers in a folder and planned to have her students recopy their papers and make the indicated corrections the following day. She had learned that revision is an important phase of the writing

It All Depends

process and hoped that this course of action would be a productive one for her students. Finally, she put some materials in her briefcase and walked to the parking lot, her previous despondency replaced with a glimmer of hopefulness.

QUESTIONS FOR REFLECTION

1. What are the key issues presented in this case?
2. What strengths did Krista demonstrate throughout the case?
3. What faulty practices or ideas did Krista demonstrate?
4. What might be some explanations about why past-tense verbs and prepositions might be especially problematic for Krista's students?
5. What strategies might you suggest to Krista to increase the likelihood that her students will apply concepts she has taught not only in language arts but in other subjects as well?

EXTENSION ACTIVITIES

1. Interview several teachers of the deaf in a variety of self-contained settings and find out what materials they use to teach written language skills.
2. Interview several resource room or itinerant teachers of the deaf. Find out how they mediate texts (if they are used) and support written language instruction for deaf students in mainstreamed settings.
3. Obtain a copy of *Teaching for Transfer: Fostering Generalization in Learning* by Anne McKeough, Judy Lupart, and Anthony Marini. If this is a problem, obtain an educational psychology textbook and find "transfer" in the index. Identify the types of transfer, factors that affect transfer, and effective procedures teachers can use to enhance transfer of learning.

Case 6: EXERCISES IN FUTILITY

4. Try to obtain a written language lesson plan from a teacher of the deaf, or observe a teacher who is working on writing proficiency with deaf students. Identify steps in the lesson that were designed to enhance transfer of the language skills into students' writing.
5. Identify materials specially designed to help deaf and hard of hearing students develop language and writing skills.

Case 7: First Things First

Suzanne Harris is enjoying her first year of teaching in a second grade class in a residential school for deaf and hard of hearing students. She is especially pleased with her reading program. She primarily uses a series of reading comprehension workbooks with short passages intended to develop basic skills such as sequencing and locating information. By doing so, she ensures that she covers the state-mandated reading standards at the second grade level. In addition, every Friday, she has her students read a variety of trade books designed to enrich their reading experience. The students are good readers and eagerly anticipate Fridays when they can read what they call "real" books.

Suzanne was looking forward to the first formal observation of her instruction by the principal, Jay Ashfield, who had been a reading specialist for many years before pursuing a degree in Educational Leadership and becoming an administrator. She was glad that he chose to come today, Friday, for the evaluation, because she planned to have her students read Joseph Bruchac's *The First Strawberries: A Cherokee Story*. The plot of this legend about the origin of strawberries involves a woman who leaves after becoming angry with her husband for speaking harshly to her. He chases her but loses ground. Because he is sorry for his behavior, the sun decides to help the man by causing blueberries and blackberries to grow, hoping the woman will stop to pick them, allowing the husband to gain ground. Unimpressed, she continues to walk. Finally, the sun causes strawberries to grow. The woman stops to try one. The sweet taste reminds her of the good times she and her husband shared. While she pauses to gather more, he catches up with her and asks her to forgive him. She responds by sharing the fruit she has gathered.

On the Friday of the observation, Suzanne did not alter her daily procedures. She completed the morning routines she usually

It All Depends

conducts with her students, at which time the principal arrived and, inconspicuously, took a seat in the back of the classroom. The timing was perfect, because Suzanne had just seated herself in front of the students and was getting ready to introduce the book they would be reading.

She held up the book and asked a student, Lisa, to sign the title. When she finished, Lisa added that she didn't like strawberries, preferring blueberries instead. Another student, Dennis, interjected that apples were his favorite fruit. Feeling the need to keep the lesson focused, Suzanne redirected students to the book she was holding up and called on two other students to sign the names of the author and illustrator. She followed this routine each Friday because, with deaf students, she felt that it made sense to set the reading process in motion by highlighting what the students could see. Then, she passed out copies of the book and instructed the students to begin reading.

After reading the story with rapt attention, the students began to raise their heads, indicating they were ready to discuss the story. At Suzanne's school, each elementary teacher is given a variety of posters that would frame post-reading discussions. Teachers are expected to use two posters, one for story details and one for the main idea. For the former, Suzanne chose the "Sequence Train," which contained the words *first, middle,* and *end* placed in the engine, car, and caboose of a train, respectively. For the latter, she selected the "Main Idea Feet," a poster on which specific details were represented by individual toes, leading to the ultimate identification of a main idea or main ideas on the soles of the feet.

As she pointed to the "Sequence Train," students raised their hands and volunteered to tell various parts of the story, which they did sequentially and accurately. Suzanne was immensely pleased. Unfortunately, the students did not do as well with the main idea. As she probed, they identified main characters, the setting, and a host of details. However, they failed to capture the main idea, theme, or key concepts supported by the details they shared. Suzanne concluded the lesson by praising them for their participation and their understanding of what happened in the story. She also encouraged them to draw their favorite scenes from the story when they went to art class, where the instructional aide would now be accompanying them.

The art period provided Suzanne with the first of two scheduled times for planning in the day. The second time was after lunch when the students went to physical education class. Today, part of her first planning period would be used for her post-observation conference. Except for the little hiccup when trying to extract the main idea of the story, she felt confident about the lesson and walked to the back of the classroom to receive the principal's feedback.

As she had anticipated, the principal had positive things to say about the students' grasp of factual information and concerns about their inability to grasp the overall theme of the story, a major skill in reading. He mentioned that *The First Strawberries: A Cherokee Story* was one of his favorite children's books, and he would have loved to see the students discuss the ideas of forgiveness and resolving conflict or how objects and sensory input can trigger powerful memories. One of the shortcomings of the lesson, in his estimation, was an absence of prereading activities that would have guided students towards these "big ideas." She simply had students begin reading the story. Principal Ashfield suggested that incorporating some prereading activities would be beneficial in helping the students not only identify facts in the story but also pick up on larger concepts that are pivotal to understanding the main ideas and themes of narrative and expository texts. Suzanne stated that she would include this prereading phase next week. They decided that he would return for a follow-up visit the following Friday for the specific purpose of observing her use of prereading activities. She thanked him for the feedback, they shook hands, and he exited the classroom.

Reflecting on the conference, Suzanne was somewhat mystified by the prereading suggestion, because she always started the reading sessions by having students identify the title, author, and illustrator of the book. Didn't these qualify as prereading? After all, this process occurs before students begin reading. Then, all of a sudden, she remembered something from one of her literacy courses—that prereading activities help to build students' background knowledge when information is unfamiliar to them.

It All Depends

With this recollection, she came up with a prereading idea for next week's story, *Frog and Toad Are Friends*. This book portrays the kindness demonstrated between the two amphibians as they share many adventures together. She anticipated that, during the allocated time, her students would be able to complete two of the five stories in the book. Since her students, like most people, probably did not know the difference between a toad and a frog, she would begin the lesson with a Venn diagram and explain the similarities and differences between the two types of amphibians. She smiled confidently, satisfied that she had thought of a solid prereading idea, one that focused on supplying background information and not simply having students identify who wrote and illustrated the book. She eagerly anticipated her next observation—and the favorable comments she was sure to receive from her principal.

QUESTIONS FOR REFLECTION

1. What are the key issues presented in this case?
2. What is your overall assessment of Suzanne's instructional practices in reading?
3. What is your assessment of Suzanne's comprehension of the purpose of prereading activities?
4. What are two prereading strategies Suzanne might have used for *The First Strawberries: A Cherokee Story*?
5. Do you think the Venn diagram idea she plans to use for *Frog and Toad Are Friends* will garner favorable feedback from her principal? Why or why not? If your answer is <u>yes</u>, explain your rationale. If your answer is <u>no</u>, identify a prereading activity you think would be more effective, and explain why.

Case 7: FIRST THINGS FIRST

Extension Activities

1. State as many goals as you can that prereading activities are intended to accomplish.
2. Using print and Internet resources, identify some prereading strategies. Categorize each strategy as to whether it is appropriate for "Narrative Text," "Expository Text," or "Both."
3. Contact teachers of the deaf at different grade levels, and find out what prereading strategies they use in the elementary school, middle school, and high school grades.

Case 8: Get It In Writing

Daniel Templer is a sixth-grade language arts teacher in a day school program in a large city in the Midwest. He is an avid tennis player and has appeared in the local newspaper for winning a couple of community-based tournaments. He encourages his students to get actively involved in community recreation activities. Because all of his students have some residual hearing and intelligible speech, these activities provide them with a way of interacting with their hearing peers and provide them with opportunities to develop coping and problem-solving skills when communicating with others, aided by the fact that they are in high-context situations. He points out to parents in a beginning-of-the-year newsletter that there are both social and communication benefits to such involvement.

Eleven-year-old Eric Shale is in Daniel's English language arts class and in his homeroom, the last period of the day. A cochlear implant user, Eric is a bright boy who underestimates his ability to be understood when he speaks. Since being implanted at age seven, he has received speech training in school. In addition, his parents have paid for private speech therapy several times a week. The intervention has yielded benefits. Other than occasional problems with consonant blends and a tendency to substitute the *sh* sound for *ch*, he is generally understood well by strangers as well as those acquainted with him.

One day during homeroom, Eric approached Daniel and told him he was interested in tennis. He stated that, in a community newsletter, he had read that a tennis pro had begun to offer lessons for children at the tennis courts in his subdivision. He said he was reluctant to sign up, specifying two areas of concern. First, he was worried about not understanding the tennis pro. Second, he was anxious about break times when the other children might try to talk with him.

It All Depends

To allay Eric's apprehension, Daniel explained that instruction would be primarily visual, with the tennis pro demonstrating the skills first. He suggested that during the drills, Eric should position himself third or fourth in line, so that he could see what was expected. Eric's nods indicated that he found this suggestion reasonable. Next, Daniel said the other children would see his cochlear implant, know that he had difficulty hearing, and would figure out ways to communicate with him if verbal interaction broke down. He also encouraged Eric to initiate communication with some of the other children. Eric vigorously shook his head and said, "No way!" Daniel asked him if he knew how to properly start and maintain conversations. Eric thought for a moment and responded, "Not really." Daniel said that was something they could discuss at some point.

The following day, Friday, was Eric's birthday. Daniel had made it standard practice to give each of the students in his homeroom a birthday card and a gift relevant to their interests. Ten minutes before the school day ended, Daniel presented Eric with his gift, a mug with two tennis racquets on it. Eric was delighted with the mug and held it up for his classmates to see as they sang and signed "Happy Birthday." The atmosphere was filled with laughter and good cheer, an enjoyable way to end the school week.

Monday morning, Daniel began language arts class with 10 minutes of journal writing. Eric asked if he could write something else. Daniel nodded his approval. His purpose for this time was simply to have his students develop writing fluency. After the students put away their journals, Eric handed Daniel his writing product, a makeshift greeting card, a sheet of paper that had been folded over twice. On the front, in capital letters, the words "THANK YOU" were written. Inside the card, Eric had written this message:

Dear Mr. Templer

Thank you for brithday card. I like you very musch. you are my frist teach give me gift. I start my tennis lesson this week. thank you for mug.

I enjoyed see your picture in newspapers. I,m glad that you are famous.

Love
Eric

Case 8: GET IT IN WRITING

Daniel was glad to know that Eric was forging ahead with his tennis lessons. Additionally, he was inordinately pleased that Eric was initiating use of his written language skills and writing with a purpose.

Later in the day, during his planning time, Daniel received a telephone call from his principal, Helen Cho, who informed him that an IEP conference for Eric had been scheduled for the following Monday. She wanted to know if he could provide Eric with a verbal or pictorial prompt to elicit a writing sample. In Eric's file were SAT-9 scores, but it was school policy to write IEP language goals based on qualitative and quantitative analysis of a written language sample for older students. Based on the writing sample, she wanted Daniel to identify strengths and weaknesses as well as compute three quantitative measures: Mean Sentence Length, T-Unit Length, and Type-Token Ratio.

The card from Eric was on the desk in front of Daniel, who thought it might be a suitable data source for the task that Helen Cho had asked him to complete. Daniel asked her if the card would be an acceptable writing sample. She replied that if he could use it to determine the specific information that was needed, it would be fine. He assured her that, by the end of the week, he would be able to supply her with the information she had requested. After the conversation, Daniel decided not to postpone the inevitable. He opened Eric's card and picked up a pen. As he poised the pen near the top of the yellow legal pad in front of him, he wondered where to begin. Finally, he resolved to get the ball rolling by accentuating the positive and starting with Eric's strengths.

QUESTIONS FOR REFLECTION

1. What are the key issues in this case?
2. What is your overall assessment of Daniel Templer as a teacher?
3. What are the benefits and disadvantages of using prompted writing products for assessment purposes?
4. What are the benefits and disadvantages of using students' spontaneous writing for assessment purposes?

It All Depends

5. Based on Eric's writing sample, answer the following questions:
   - What are his strengths? need areas?
   - What is the Mean Sentence Length?
   - What is the Type-Token Ratio?
   - What is the T-Unit Length?
6. In a conversation with Eric, Daniel identified weaknesses in the area of communication as they relate to social skills. Would you characterize these as learning needs that would be the responsibility of the language arts teacher? Why or why not?

EXTENSION ACTIVITIES

1. Collect a writing sample from a student, and assess it with respect to its strengths and weaknesses. Also, calculate the Type-Token Ratio, Mean Sentence Length, and T-Unit Length of the sample.
2. The quantitative measures Type-Token Ratio, Mean Sentence Length, and T-Unit Length have been used in this case. What is the purpose of each of these measures?
3. Contact a curriculum specialist. Find out whether or not his or her program systematically monitors the language growth of its students. If so, identify the specific procedures that are used to gather data and document progress.
4. Identify five language assessment tools used with students who are deaf and hard of hearing. For each assessment, identify the specific aspect(s) of language (e.g., vocabulary, semantics, syntax, and morphology) that it targets and briefly describe how the assessment is carried out.
5. The ultimate purpose of language assessment is instructional planning, which can be facilitated by resources. Identify language resources for deaf and hard of hearing students, and relate them to the specific component of language (e.g., vocabulary, syntax, and spelling) each resource would be helpful in developing or remediating.

Case 9: Poetic License

Emlyn Pratt is a first-year seventh-grade teacher in a residential program in the Northeast. Her students participate in the general curriculum. In college, she was a dual major: Deaf Education and English. In fact, she was an English major initially and added Deaf Education to her program of study when she took a sign language for non-majors course as a General Education elective and became fascinated with manual communication. Also, she seemed to have a knack for learning it. Soon thereafter, she set her sights on a teaching career in which she could share her love of English language arts through the air with deaf students.

When Emlyn arrived at school on Wednesday morning, the principal explained that Mr. Brant Unsworth, the father of one of her students, wanted to sit in on his son's English language arts class during third period. Emlyn was both anxious and excited: anxious because she had never had a parent visit during a class session; excited because she was introducing a poetry unit that she was certain her students would find enlightening and enjoyable. She had decided to make Carl Sandburg's "The Fog" the focal point of her lesson. First, at six lines, it was short enough to cover in a single class period and allow for multiple readings. Second, the poem lent itself to visualization. Third, fog was a relatable concept, increasing the likelihood that making metaphorical connections would not be a struggle for students. Finally, it could be used to promote the mastery of Common Core State Standards such as demonstrating comprehension of figurative language and analyzing how a poem's structure contributes to its meaning.

On the day of the lesson, Emlyn began by showing a fog bank on the interactive whiteboard and had students brainstorm associations. They did so energetically. Next, she displayed "The Fog" and directed students to read it silently to themselves. Next, she signed

It All Depends

the poem expressively after which the students signed the poem chorally as she led them. Then, she asked the students if they noticed that Sandburg gave the fog the ability to move as if it were a living thing. Scanning the poem once more, the students responded with a chorus of nods. Emlyn labeled the concept *personification* and proceeded to give students additional examples. Finally, she led the class in a discussion of the meaning that Sandburg was trying to convey.

To follow up on the lesson development, she had the students do an application activity in which they used "The Fog" as a model to compose their own poems based on some element of nature such as rain or wind. Before the end of the class period, several students shared their poems, which admirably incorporated personification. As the students were departing, Emlyn felt a tremendous sense of accomplishment, because her two primary objectives had been met. Her students had discussed the meaning of the poem "The Fog" and demonstrated comprehension of personification by applying this concept in their own poems.

When the last student had departed, she pulled up a chair next to Mr. Unsworth's chair and asked if he had any questions. She was not quite sure what to expect in response. However, she was utterly astounded when he gave her a scornful look and asked caustically, "Since deaf students have so many problems with writing sentences that are grammatically correct, why are you wasting their time on poetry when it would be better spent on grammar or something else that might be more practical?"

Taken aback, Emlyn had just gone from an extreme high to an extreme low, much like the sudden 200-foot vertical drop she had experienced on a diving coaster ride at a Florida amusement park. However, that was all about fun. This situation? Well, not so much. She rarely found herself at a loss for words, and his question hung in the air for a long moment as she struggled to maintain her presence of mind and her professionalism while mentally crafting a thoughtful, appropriate response to what she viewed as a thoughtless, inappropriate question. Although she was livid, she heeded an inner voice advising her to hold her emotions in check. Accordingly,

Case 9: POETIC LICENSE

she resolved to be strong, deciding that Mr. Unsworth would not undermine her integrity as a professional teacher. And with a surge of inner strength, she regained her composure and broke the silence. Unflinchingly, she raised her gaze to his and confidently responded to the question that had been posed to her.

QUESTIONS FOR REFLECTION

1. What are the key issues presented in the case?
2. Evaluate Emlyn's lesson in terms of content, planning, delivery, and assessment of student learning.
3. How might Emlyn respond to Mr. Unsworth's question in terms of its *affective* content (the concern expressed about deaf students' literacy levels) and its *substantive* content (his assertion regarding the impracticality of teaching poetry to deaf students)?
4. What are several useful guidelines to consider whenever parents visit during a class session for any reason?

EXTENSION ACTIVITIES

1. Access an online poetry resource, and identify two ideas for teaching poetry, noting adaptations that might be necessary for helping deaf and hard of hearing students understand sound-based poetic devices such as iambs, alliteration, and onomatopoeia.
2. In bilingual education and general education, using poetry to teach grammar is an approach sometimes used for language study. Do an online search, and identify two strategies that might be useful in deaf education.
3. There are many online articles on working successfully with challenging parents. Access several of them, and identify five suggestions that you think are especially beneficial. Try to include these areas in your response:
    - defusing negative emotions
    - engaging in perspective taking

It All Depends

- displaying effective communication skills
- maintaining professionalism
- concluding the interaction

Case 10: Put to the Test

In his Deaf Education courses, Anton Landau had learned that deaf and hard of hearing students tend to perform poorly on formal writing assessments. As a high school English language arts teacher, he was determined that such would not be the case for his sophomores, who would be taking the state writing assessment in the spring. He had seven months to prepare his students to do well on the assessment. He was teaching in a bi-bi program. All of his students had at least one deaf parent and were proficient users of ASL. Since their elementary years, students had learned translation strategies and, as a result, were adept at code-switching between ASL through the air and English in print.

In addition to continuing to implement ASL-English translation learning experiences, Anton capitalized on his students' intense interest in reading. He took great pleasure in introducing his students to the classic literature he had enjoyed as a high school student. They were in the midst of reading the short story "The Gift of the Magi," with the novels *The Grapes of Wrath* and *To Kill a Mockingbird* on the reading list for the remainder of the academic year. Anton's plan was to use these novels not only as the basis for reading comprehension but also as mentor texts, selecting excerpts displaying specific writing concepts and having his students produce writing in those styles. This integration of reading and writing was consistent with the concept of balanced literacy, which, he had learned in his teacher education program, was an effective approach for guiding students' English language arts instruction. In addition, throughout the semester, he gave priority to sentence structure, because he wanted to ensure that the writing his students produced was comprehensible and coherent.

In April, as his students were administered the state writing assessment, Anton felt confident about their performance. The last

It All Depends

day of school, their writing scores arrived. To his chagrin, his students collectively had not performed as well as he had hoped. He immediately visited the school's literacy coach, Blair Serna-Collins, and explained the situation. She pointed out that she had worked for many years as a specialist supporting teachers of the deaf and found that they often focused on sentence structure and grammar almost to the exclusion of other features of writing. She emphasized that the state evaluated student compositions based on the six traits of writing. Anton indicated that he had heard of this model but admitted he had not used it specifically as a framework for his writing instruction. Blair went to a nearby file cabinet and extracted a folder. From it, she took out two copies of the six traits and handed one of them to Anton. As he was perusing it, she explained that his initial approach may have, in fact, produced gains in sentence fluency and conventions, because they were the areas he stressed. Furthermore, she noted that his students practiced modeling narrative text excerpts. The narrative genre was evaluated at only the elementary level.

Before concluding their meeting to participate in a webinar, Blair encouraged Anton to carve out some time over the summer to think of lessons that would develop students' proficiency with content, organization, voice, and word choice to complement his current focus on sentence structure and conventions. She stood, shook his hand cordially, and predicted, "I believe this time next year, we'll be having a different conversation about your students' writing assessment results."

Walking back to his classroom, Anton was pleased with Blair's guidance and gladdened by her encouraging words. She had mentioned summer, and he knew at least two activities that his would include: surfing and collecting—surfing the web for writing ideas and collecting strategies for developing the six traits of writing.

Case 10: PUT TO THE TEST

Questions for Reflection

1. What are the key issues presented in the case?
2. Evaluate Anton's use of mentor texts as a component of his overall approach to writing instruction for his sophomores.
3. What do you think is the proper emphasis on grammar and syntax within the context of writing instruction?
4. What are three specific ways that teachers can help prepare students for statewide writing assessments?

Extension Activities

1. Many school districts and states have adopted Six Traits as their writing instruction framework. Search online and do the following: (a) specify what each of the six traits encompasses and (b) identify one strategy that can be used for developing each of the traits.
2. There are frameworks for writing instruction other than Six Traits. Search online, locate one of them, and summarize its approach to teaching and improving student writing.
3. Access three states' assessment websites. Contrast the writing genres and formats expected of elementary students and secondary students.

Part 3:
Content Instruction

Case 11: Cultural Literacy

Ethan Finley is a first-year teacher in a self-contained classroom located at a public school. He teaches six fifth-grade students. Four of the students are profoundly deaf and use sign language to communicate. The other two students have mild hearing losses, but both were enrolled early in residential programs, where they developed satisfactory sign language skills. There is an FM system in the classroom, and Ethan uses Simultaneous Communication to teach his students. This approach seems to meet the communication needs of all six students.

While Ethan is answerable to the principal for general employment matters, he is supervised in curriculum and instruction by the county's Deaf & Hard of Hearing Program Specialist, Marie Shapiro. He feels very fortunate, because she is hard of hearing and has direct knowledge about having a hearing loss. She has a profoundly deaf cousin with whom she spent a lot of time growing up. From her cousin, she learned sign language. She is an excellent signer and, from personal and professional experiences, knows a great deal about speech and amplification.

Since beginning his job two months ago, Ethan has been punctual in submitting his lesson plans. In addition to detailing his instructional methods, he makes sure that he shows how his lesson objectives relate to state curriculum standards. At the orientation for new teachers, the district superintendent emphasized that, like veteran teachers, new teachers were expected to adhere to a standards-based instructional model, the standards being those identified in the state curriculum frameworks.

Marie Shapiro has always indicated that Ethan's lesson plans, which he e-mails to her weekly, are satisfactory. A few times, however, she has suggested that he consider incorporating Deaf studies. He plans to develop a unit on Deaf culture eventually, but for the

It All Depends

time being, he feels a need to focus on teaching the state standards the superintendent stressed so heavily during the orientation.

Recently, Marie Shapiro scheduled her first formal observation of Ethan's instruction. In anticipating the visit, he felt generally prepared for the English language arts and social studies classes she would be observing. He felt a little bit anxious, but he told himself this feeling was natural and was able to calm himself down. She had chosen the two classes at the end of the school day so that she could have a post-observation conference without interfering with another class session or a scheduled planning period.

When Marie Shapiro entered, the students noticed her two hearing aids immediately and became animated, asking her a steady stream of questions. After answering questions about her hearing loss, she explained the purpose of her visit and encouraged the students to give Mr. Finley their undivided attention. They nodded assent.

At the conclusion of the two classes, Ethan thanked the students for their attention and involvement, and told them they needed to copy the homework assignments from the board before they left. As they did so, Ethan quickly reflected on the lessons. He thought they had gone well. More important, he felt confident the students had achieved the two state standards. In English language arts, they had *discussed technologies to enhance the efficiency and effectiveness of communication*. In social studies, they had *identified laws and government systems since the Renaissance*.

After the students left, Marie Shapiro began her assessment. She was extremely complimentary about his communication skills and instructional procedures, which maintained high levels of student engagement. Her only suggestion was that he should seize opportunities to incorporate Deaf studies into his instruction on an ongoing basis. She emphasized the need for his students to meet and learn about deaf adults and the important contributions they have made—and are continuing to make—to society, visual communication aids, and legislation designed to provide access for people with a hearing loss. She underscored the particular importance of doing so in a public school placement, where there is limited opportunity for incidental contact with deaf adults who can serve as role models.

Case 11: CULTURAL LITERACY

Regular attention to Deaf studies would help to foster individual and group identity, she maintained.

Ethan agreed but quickly pointed out the superintendent's mandate for addressing state standards. Clarifying that she was not requesting that Ethan disregard the superintendent's message, Marie Shapiro smiled and stated that he could, in fact, do both. She suggested an infusion approach. Observing his puzzlement, she pointed out that in his English language arts lesson, he mentioned many technologies but did not include TTYs, hearing aids, cochlear implants, FM systems, wireless pagers, closed captioning, or real-time captioning, all of which have significance in the lives of deaf and hard of hearing individuals. Including this technology, she said, would not have contravened the state standard he was expected to teach. In his social studies lesson, she registered surprise that, although a number of major laws were discussed, he had failed to include the Individuals with Disabilities Education Act (IDEA) or the Americans with Disabilities Act (ADA), both of which had current and future significance in the lives of his students. Again, she stressed that discussion of this legislation would not have compromised the state standard being taught.

Ethan said he understood what she meant by increasing his attention to Deaf studies without decreasing attention to state standards. She explained that it is, obviously, not possible to do so with every standard, but there are more opportunities for infusion than he might think. Then, she asked to see some of the standards he planned to teach the following week. He gave her a sheet with a list of some of the standards. She took a moment to peruse them, placed an asterisk next to two of them, and stated that they would lend themselves to the infusion of Deaf studies, which she would look for in his next set of lesson plans. She returned the paper to him, and he glanced at the two standards she had designated:

*Students will distinguish between fact and opinion. (social studies)
*Students will know selected scientists and their accomplishments. (science)

It All Depends

Ethan thanked Marie Shapiro for her observation and feedback, and she once again commended him on a job well done. As she was leaving, he felt pleased that everything had gone so well. Almost immediately, that delight was tempered with a trace of apprehension about how he would incorporate Deaf studies into the plans that he would submit to her next week for the lessons related to the social studies and science standards she had identified.

QUESTIONS FOR REFLECTION

1. What are the key issues presented in this case?
2. How might Deaf studies be infused into the science and social studies standards highlighted by Marie Shapiro?
3. How might a teacher incorporate Deaf studies into a class that has students whose hearing losses range from slight to profound?
4. What are the advantages and disadvantages of a stand-alone approach to teaching Deaf studies in a separate unit?
5. What are the advantages and disadvantages of an infusion approach to teaching Deaf studies?
6. How might a teacher in a public school address the need for deaf role models in a setting in which deaf employees are a rarity?

EXTENSION ACTIVITIES

1. Review the curriculum frameworks in the state in which you plan to teach. Identify standards in a variety of subject areas. Indicate how Deaf studies might be infused into each standard.
2. Contact teachers of the deaf in different educational settings and at different educational levels. Determine how they expose their students to Deaf studies.
3. Teachers often establish special-interest learning centers in their classrooms. Identify 10 resources (books, magazines, videotapes, DVDs, CD-ROMs, websites, or artifacts) you would include in a

Case 11: CULTURAL LITERACY

Deaf studies learning center to enlighten students about deafness in these areas: American Sign Language, and communication with technology, history, culture, literature, and the arts.

Case 12: A Textbook Example

Garrett Wynter is a first-year itinerant teacher. He applied for this job because it has a dimension he enjoys greatly: variety. There are two itinerant teachers in his district, one for elementary students and the other for secondary students. Garrett's responsibility is the latter. His caseload consists of 20 middle and high school students. Most of his time is spent consulting with the general education teachers. Sometimes, however, at the students' request, he will provide direct assistance, usually in the form of brief tutorials that will help them clarify and get started on an assignment, or help them with study skills.

Garrett and the other itinerant teacher both graduated in May from the same university with majors in Deaf Education & Elementary Education. When they applied for the two vacancies, they realized that if they both were hired, one of them would be in a position that dealt with an age group that was not the primary focus of their undergraduate program. When the decision was made that he would have the secondary itinerant position, Garrett viewed his employment status with mixed emotions: glad to be employed and working with deaf students; uneasy that he might encounter situations for which he felt unprepared.

Apprehension was what Garrett was feeling before—and after—a meeting with the science and social studies teachers of Bryce DeCamp, one of his eighth-grade students. It was the end of the first quarter grading period, and Bryce had not performed well in these courses. Garrett had decided to meet with the two teachers to gather their perspectives on why Bryce had done poorly and, more important, how he could support their instruction and help Bryce achieve different outcomes for the second quarter.

Madeline Kessler, the science teacher, began the discussion. Her overall assessment was that Bryce needed some textbook reading instruction. She stated that he seemed to be a good reader and

It All Depends

responded satisfactorily to literal questions, but he did not process information at deeper levels or perceive the connections between concepts and ideas. This observation was borne out by his performance on the most recent text-based assessment. He responded to factual questions well but failed to respond adequately to items requiring him to analyze or synthesize information.

The social studies teacher, Franklin Cohen, agreed with Madeline's observations. He stated that generally Bryce needed help in developing study skills for textbook reading assignments, adding that these skills would be useful not only this year but also next year. When Bryce was ready to enter high school, the number of textbook assignments expected to be completed independently in class or as homework would increase. Franklin had noticed two major problems in his social studies class: identifying relevant information and organizing that information. Franklin's practice was to require his students to outline each major section of each chapter. Bryce often included irrelevant details and thus had difficulties in organizing the information in any logical or meaningful way.

Before concluding the meeting, both Madeline and Franklin made it clear that they felt Bryce was a capable student who, with help in textbook reading, could enhance his reading comprehension and, in turn, achieve better grades. They also commented favorably on Bryce's self-advocacy. One day after class, through the educational interpreter, he expressed concern about his grades to both teachers, saying he studied his textbooks on a regular basis. When Madeline asked how he studied, his response was that he "read" the chapters. When probed about the type of notes he took while reading, he indicated that he didn't have to take notes, because he had a fantastic memory. The teachers told him they would consult with Mr. Wynter, who would work on some strategies to assist him.

After Madeline and Franklin left, Garrett received a text message from Bryce, who wanted to meet with him during homeroom, the last period of the day. When Bryce arrived, he was clearly upset as they discussed his grades in science and social studies. Garrett assured him that he would come up with a plan to reverse this unfortunate situation. They planned to meet three times a week to work on specific strategies to help Bryce with tests and assignments. The word *assignments* reminded Bryce of a summary on economic systems he had written that was due to Mr. Cohen the next week. Since they had planned the first tutorial for Monday, Bryce said that Garrett could look at it over the weekend and give him some feedback then. Garret commended Bryce on his sensible suggestion and took the summary.

When Bryce left, Garrett reflected on his promise to come up with some strategies to turn his grades around. Now all he had to do was deliver. Before packing his briefcase to leave for the day, Garrett quickly perused the summary Bryce had given him. Even though it had been years since he had studied economic systems, he knew immediately that the paragraph did not contain key information. Also, the sentences were not organized in a way that was consistent with classifying information. Given the problems Madeline and Franklin had identified, Garrett felt that he had a starting point. If only he could figure out what to do next. He walked to his car, keenly aware of what would occupy a large portion of his weekend.

On his drive home, Garrett racked his brain, reflecting on what he had learned in his language courses. Through his mind streamed memories of shared reading, predictable books, and big books, none of which seemed applicable to Bryce's issues with middle school texts. However, as he continued to drive, something nagged at the edges of his consciousness, something about texts. All of a sudden, it hit him. In a language course, he had learned about expository text structures, how subject matter text is organized. A data chart would be useful for helping Bryce to better categorize information about economic systems. Then, it could be used as a prewriting activity to write a more effective summary.

One of Garrett's favorite quotations came to mind: "The man who moves mountains begins by carrying stones." Sure, he realized that he would also have to investigate some relevant study skills and other content literacy strategies but, for now, he was heartened by the fact that he was ready for his tutoring session on Monday, ready to move one stone of the mountain that proved to be an obstacle for Bryce. Garrett also was encouraged by the fact that the strategies he

It All Depends

would use to help Bryce could also be used with other deaf students with similar content literacy needs. Perhaps, he thought expectantly, working with secondary deaf students would not be as formidable as he had once thought.

QUESTIONS FOR REFLECTION

1. What are the key issues presented in this case?
2. Garrett decided to start his tutoring sessions with Bryce with work on expository text structure. Do you think this instruction will be beneficial in remedying Bryce's problem with writing summaries? Why or why not?
3. Based on the assessment of Bryce's science and social studies teachers, what are three priority needs (other than summary writing) that Garrett should address? For each priority need you identified, suggest strategies that might be helpful in meeting that need.

EXTENSION ACTIVITIES

1. Contact several teachers of the deaf at various grade levels, and find out the types of reading their students are expected to do. Try to make some generalizations about the nature and demands of reading tasks at these levels: lower elementary (K–2), upper elementary (3–5), middle school (6–8), and high school (9–12).
2. Access the curriculum frameworks for the state in which you plan to pursue employment upon graduation. Determine whether or not specific study skills are reflected in the state standards and, if so, at what grade levels they are expected to be taught.
3. Examine your own teacher education program. In what course or courses were you taught strategies for developing study skills, learning strategies, and content literacy, particularly those expected at the secondary level?

Case 13: A Word to the Wise

Hannah Silva is a first-year resource teacher in a middle school in a rural community. In the school, there are nine deaf and hard of hearing students: three sixth graders, two seventh graders, and four eighth graders. With these students, she works primarily on study skills. The Coordinator of Low Incidence Programs suggested this course of action for two reasons. First, these students will soon be in high school, where they will be expected to assume greater levels of academic independence. Second, these skills also will be beneficial to them now: From time to time, one of the students requests assistance on a specific assignment or project.

While she observes the students in their classrooms on a regular basis and provides consultation to their general education teachers, Hannah especially appreciates having teachers identify specific problems students are experiencing, because some academic challenges are not readily apparent during a classroom observation. This was the case recently regarding her two seventh graders, Molly and Caleb. Both are hard of hearing and have bilateral hearing losses. They know basic signs that they have picked up when interacting with the other students on campus. Larry Reynolds, their science teacher, and Denise Rayne, their social studies teacher, paid a visit to Hannah.

Larry and Denise expressed their belief that both Molly and Caleb could improve their grades in science and social studies if they had a better grasp of the vocabulary for these classes. Their reading skills were satisfactory, but both teachers speculated that even their reading comprehension would improve if their vocabularies did.

Hannah requested specifics about the students' vocabulary difficulties. Larry indicated that both students seemed to know the key terms on a single level, not really understanding how context changes word meanings. Denise stated that when her social studies

It All Depends

students were discussing *consumers* and asked the meaning of the word, Caleb excitedly raised his hand and provided a textbook definition: *animals that obtain food by preying on other organisms.* Larry smiled and interjected that the day before, they had discussed consumers and producers in his science class. He added that when his class was studying vertebrate groups, Molly had offered an accurate definition of *amphibians,* but later identified lizards, turtles, and eels as examples.

Hannah said that she had time for one more example, because a student would be arriving in a few minutes for assistance. Larry stated that on a quiz on plant parts, both students identified the meaning of *sepal,* properly identifying its position at the bottom of a plant. However, on an illustration of a plant, one of them labeled it in the middle of the diagram, and one of them placed it near the top. So there seemed to be a discrepancy between recognizing vocabulary and real understanding.

Hannah thanked them both for their concerns, said that she wished more of her students' teachers would take such initiative, and assured them that she would lend support to the instruction they provided by working on content-specific vocabulary with Molly and Caleb. To help in this endeavor, Hannah asked them to e-mail her key terms that would be used in the next units they planned to teach. They both said they would and left.

By the end of the day, Hannah had received the vocabulary information she had requested. She felt that she was so fortunate to have colleagues like Denise and Larry, who were willing to do their part in helping her meet her students' educational needs. In science, the students would be doing a unit on rocks, with key vocabulary being the following: *mineral, gem, metal, volcano, lava, magnet, gravel, coal, rust,* and *crystal.* In social studies, the next unit would be on maps and globes. Denise provided these key terms: *scale, legend, symbol, equator, hemisphere, latitude, longitude, boundary, elevation,* and *landmark.*

Hannah felt good having a week to preteach the vocabulary. It gave her adequate time to have Molly and Caleb do a variety of activities. The first thing she did was provide them with dictionaries and have them copy the definition of each word. This task took two days.

Case 13: A WORD TO THE WISE

Then, knowing that students need repetition for vocabulary development, the following two days, she had the students do different worksheets she had developed. She had incorporated the words into word searches and crossword puzzles to increase their sight familiarity with the words and ensure they knew the meanings. On Friday, she had the students match the 20 words with their definitions. She was ecstatic that both students had made perfect scores.

Two weeks later, Hannah saw Denise and Larry in the cafeteria and went over to sit with them. Even though teachers don't generally like to talk shop during lunch, she was hoping to get an update on Caleb and Molly. When she broached the topic, by the way that Denise and Larry looked uncomfortably at each other, Hannah was sure she had her answer. They both admitted that the situation with Caleb and Molly had not changed noticeably. Both students, while obviously familiar with the words, still seemed to lack a conceptual understanding of them.

Dismayed but determined, Hannah apologetically assured them that she would continue to tutor the students and try some other strategies. Sensing Hannah's uneasiness, Larry and Denise quickly changed the topic. However, the discussion about the latest current event existed simply as background noise. Hannah had only one thing on her mind: vocabulary strategies that would be more effective for Caleb and Molly.

QUESTIONS FOR REFLECTION

1. What are the key issues raised in this case?
2. What is your speculation about the reasons Molly and Caleb are having difficulty with the vocabulary for the two content classes mentioned in the case?
3. What are some vocabulary strategies that would meet the specific learning needs identified in the previous question?
4. What is your assessment of the strengths and weaknesses of the approach that Hannah used to enhance the vocabulary development of Molly and Caleb?

It All Depends

5. What is your opinion of the course of action that Larry and Denise followed to improve the vocabulary development of the two deaf students in their classes?

EXTENSION ACTIVITIES

1. Consult language arts textbooks or the Internet, and identify strategies for developing the following: (a) basic sight words, (b) signal sight words, and (c) content-specific vocabulary.
2. Choose several of the science and social studies vocabulary words presented in the case and explain vocabulary activities that would be useful in teaching them.
3. Contact teachers of the deaf, and find out vocabulary strategies they use in the elementary school, middle school, and high school grades.
4. Contact two curriculum specialists. Find out what informal and/or formal tests are used to assess students' vocabulary levels.

Case 14: Bad Science

Nina Manchester is an itinerant teacher in a large school district in the Southwest. She knew she wanted to be a teacher of the deaf since the time she was in kindergarten and had a deaf girl in her class who taught everyone sign language. Seeing some of the problems her deaf classmate experienced over the years, Nina wanted not only to pursue a career in deaf education but also to cultivate a reputation as being a fierce advocate for students who are deaf and hard of hearing.

Nina's caseload consists of only secondary students. She purposely sought out an itinerant position, because she craves variety. She also loves a challenge, which is exactly what her next visit will present. She will be visiting a sophomore biology class in which the lone deaf student in it, Jarvis Parnell, had received an F on his interim report card. Nina has nothing but respect for her undergraduate teacher education program. However, truth be told: It was awesome in its language and literacy focus but not as strong on content preparation, and certainly not for the secondary level. Even though she is certified K–12, she never had even one field experience in which she worked with high school, or even middle school, students. Fortunately, she had some memorable high school learning experiences of her own to reference.

On the drive over, she reflected on her high school biology class in which active learning was standard operating procedure. She pleasantly recalled exploring taste receptors by eating jellybeans, understanding DNA analysis by collecting cheek scrapings, and learning about the alcohol fermentation in yeast, using it later to make bread. However, what she would observe during her visit diverged completely from her fond high school science memories. The teacher, Conrad Tarver, lectured the whole time as students desperately tried to take notes. The poor interpreter valiantly tried to

It All Depends

keep up. If students had questions, none dared to try and find an opening in the tightly structured, briskly paced lesson. Nina found that even she had to struggle to maintain focus.

After class, she met with Jarvis, who confirmed her surmise: that he could do better if there were visuals to accompany the lecture. And some hands-on work would be even better. Most important, Jarvis did not feel the work was beyond him, and that the F did not reflect his true ability if he had more visual access to the lesson concepts.

Nina needed to meet with Mr. Tarver. Clearly, at the very least, visuals needed to be incorporated into the lessons for Jarvis. They would, no doubt, benefit the other students as well, she thought. Perhaps that could be her approach: promoting the benefits of visual aids and active learning as beneficial for all of his students. However, she needed some research to buttress her position since, admittedly, she was not a content expert in the field of science.

Over the next two days, Nina pored over the National Science Teachers Association (NSTA) standards, as well as the Common Core State Standards, because she was well aware that there were English language arts standards in science at the secondary level. Although Nina was slightly anxious on the day of the meeting, when she approached Mr. Tarver's classroom, she felt she was as ready as she would ever be. Nonetheless, she knew she had to tread carefully. The last thing she wanted to do was set the tone for an adversarial relationship.

Nina began by broaching an interpreting issue. Yesterday, she had met with the interpreter, Duane Banta, who complained that, at the beginning of the school year, he had asked the teacher for a copy of the text or at least a list of the key vocabulary, to no avail. After two reminders, he felt that continuing to do so would simply incite the teacher's anger. Without a word, Mr. Tarver stood, walked over to a shelf, and retrieved a science text, which he handed to Nina and returned to the chair behind his desk. He said that a student had recently relocated to another state, and that the interpreter could have the extra text. So far, so good, she thought.

Case 14: BAD SCIENCE

Next, Nina underscored the visual orientation of deaf and hard of hearing students and strongly encouraged the use of graphic organizers from time to time to depict concepts and show relationships between them. She noted that the NSTA standards supported the use of graphic organizers as well as active learning, both of which would advantage not only Jarvis but also his classmates. She thought she would wait to discuss the CCSS emphasis. One victory at a time, she decided.

Mr. Tarver slowly shook his head, a disgusted look on his face. For several long moments, an awkward silence ensued. Nina was sure that he was taking time to weigh his words carefully. Finally, he gave her a glower and stated firmly, "Ms. Manchester, I know you are doing your job. And I am doing mine. I have taught biology for 20 years. There are many concepts to be covered. And at the end of each school year, I am one of only a handful of science teachers who cover all of the state standards. I believe I am competent in conveying science information to students, regardless of whether they can—or cannot—hear. Now, if you don't mind, I must prepare my lectures for tomorrow."

Mr. Tarver looked down and began searching through some papers on his desk, a gesture that Nina took to mean she had been dismissed. As she rose, not wanting the dispute to intensify, she was determined to end of a positive note. "I appreciate your time, Mr. Tarver. And thanks for the text for the interpreter." Not bothering to look up at her, he nodded curtly.

When Nina exited the building, she inhaled deeply several times. Memories of the encounter were still resonant. She needed massive doses of fresh air. Plus, she needed some time to recover and reflect. She hated this part of her job. Unfortunately, it seemed all too common for her general education colleagues to construe her consultation as criticism, and they inevitably become defensive. Just as Mr. Tarver did. Perhaps, she thought, this negativity comes with the territory. Perhaps she could have handled the situation better. Questions to ponder in the days ahead.

It All Depends

QUESTIONS FOR REFLECTION

1. What are the key issues raised in this case?
2. What are some ways that itinerant teachers can approach consultations in areas in which their professional knowledge might be lacking?
3. Evaluate Nina's approach to consulting with Mr. Tarver. What might you have done similarly? What might you have done differently?
4. What do you think the next step should be in Nina's approach with Mr. Tarver?
5. At the conclusion of the case, Nina speculated that when itinerant teachers provide feedback to general education teachers, conflicts are unavoidable or, as she put it, they "come with the territory." Do you agree or disagree? Why or why not?

EXTENSION ACTIVITIES

1. Summarize the general approaches to content area instruction (K–12) as endorsed by the major professional organizations for the three content areas identified below.
   - Mathematics (National Council of Teachers of Mathematics)
   - Science (National Science Teachers Association)
   - Social Studies (National Council for the Social Studies)
2. Search online for an itinerant teacher position. List the stated job responsibilities. Discuss which ones you feel would be relatively easy to carry out and which ones you think would be more challenging to perform. For those you have placed in the latter category, briefly explain why.
3. Workplace conflict resolution is a topic that is addressed in many online articles. Access several of them, and list at least five healthy strategies for managing and resolving conflict with colleagues to maintain a productive work environment.

Case 15: You Do the Math

Denton Perry is a resource teacher who provides instructional support for deaf and hard of hearing students in a public school setting. He addresses students' needs based on referrals by their general education teachers, who identify specific areas of academic need. Yesterday, he received a referral for Noelle Rubin, a third grader who is beginning to experience problems in mathematics. According to her teacher, Noelle's computation skills are strong; however, her ability to solve story problems is weak. She seems to simply guess at the relationship between the numbers presented in word problems.

Noelle would be coming by for assistance during homeroom time in a couple of hours. In the interim, Denton pulled a couple of story problems from a math workbook he had picked up at a local school supply store over the summer. Admittedly, Denton was somewhat anxious about this particular situation, because math had never been his strong suit. Also, to date, all of the referrals for resource room assistance had been for students having difficulties in their English language arts classes. However, he had paid enough attention in his educational measurement course in college to know that he should start with assessment and use his diagnostic observations to develop a plan of action. An involuntary smile crossed his face as he thought wistfully of Dr. Van Orden, professor in that course, who would be very proud of him right now.

Denton's nostalgic trip down Memory Lane was cut short by Noelle's entrance into his work area in one of the side rooms of the school's library. He had introduced himself to all of the deaf and hard of hearing students at the beginning of the school year. However, because this was his first time working directly with Noelle, they spent a few minutes discussing her performance in all of her subjects. She indicated that she was doing very well in English language arts, science, and social studies. She then explained that

It All Depends

math had started out fairly well, but now with story problems, she was starting to become more confused and earn lower grades. This insight provided an ideal transition to a discussion of the referral, and the fact that she would be visiting him during homeroom for a period of time to receive assistance to increase her understanding of story problems and, by extension, her math grades. Before moving on, he asked Noelle if she thought that her interpreter was signing competently in her math course, explaining that signing math concepts can sometimes be more challenging than signing concepts in other subjects. She grinned sheepishly and signed that she was sure the math, not the interpreter, was the problem.

With the preliminaries out of the way, Denton handed the math workbook to Noelle and directed her to read a story problem he had circled.

> Mrs. Farnham had $10. She bought lunch, which cost $6.50. How much money does she have left?

"So how do I know which math operation to use?" Noelle asked, after reading the problem.

Denton had a brainstorm. He grabbed eight pencils from a pencil holder on his desk and handed them to Noelle. "Count them," he said.

In short order, she signed, "Finished. Eight."

"New story problem," Denton said. He reached over and took two pencils from her. Then he continued, "Noelle had 8 pencils. Mr. Perry took 2 of them. How many pencils does Noelle have left?"

"Six," she signed. Already ahead of him, she added, "OK, the word *left* means something becomes less, which means I should subtract. So Mrs. Farnham had $3.50 left." She smiled broadly as Denton verified the accuracy of her answer.

"Wow! This is not going to be difficult for you at all," Denton assured her. "Our time is almost up, but we do have time for one more problem." He pointed to a second story problem in the workbook.

> In the 2012 Summer Olympics in London, Ryan Lochte won 5 medals, and Michael Phelps won 6 medals. How many combined medals did the 2 swimmers win?

Case 15: YOU DO THE MATH

Denton watched as Noelle signed the problem slowly and thoughtfully. Then, she surprised him with both an answer and a rationale for it. "The answer is 11. When I signed *combine*, I noticed I put my two hands together, so I put the two numbers together." She furrowed her brows, crossed her fingers, and waited for Denton's response.

He held both hands in the air and twisted them a few times. This applause in ASL cheered Noelle. Denton said, "Correct. Conceptual signing can often help to visualize the meaning of a story problem. I am very pleased with your math skills, but I am even prouder of your thinking skills. We will work on some more strategies later."

Noelle pumped her fists and smiled triumphantly. She was so motivated that she was about to request another problem. However, she saw a light begin to flash, signaling that the dismissal bell was sounding. "Thank you for your help," she signed and picked up her backpack. She hurried to the school bus loading area, more confident that math story problems might be more manageable than she had previously thought.

A short time later, Denton also left, with a similar feeling of accomplishment. He had identified three workable strategies: personalizing the story problem, noting key words, and attending to how concepts are signed. Now he just needed to identify other techniques for expanding Noelle's repertoire of strategies for math problem solving.

Heading out to his car, Denton struggled to grasp an elusive notion tugging at the periphery of his consciousness. By the time he pulled on his seat belt, it hit him. As Noelle signed the second story problem, she slowed recurrently to carefully consider the signs that would help her make sense of the print—in other words: reading comprehension. He laughed out loud, discerning his epiphany that this might be a language arts referral, after all.

It All Depends

QUESTIONS FOR REFLECTION

1. What are the key issues presented in the case?
2. Do you think Noelle's math status warranted a referral from her general education teacher? Why or why not?
3. Because they are called story problems, these problems obviously reflect a mix of reading (story) and math (problems). How might elementary teachers integrate the two disciplines so that they complement each other and benefit students?
4. In addition to the strategies that Denton identified in his first meeting with Noelle, what are four other strategies that can be used to help her solve math story problems more proficiently?

EXTENSION ACTIVITIES

1. Identify key words and phrases in math story problems that indicate when the four basic math operations should be performed. Also, include any key words that might be used to signal more than one operation.
2. Locate four websites that provide elementary and secondary students with opportunities to develop or practice their math problem solving skills.
3. There are mnemonic strategies intended to assist students with following a systematic sequence of steps for solving math problems. Many of these strategies involve acrostics, in which each letter of a word begins a sentence identifying a step to be carried out. They include CUBES, DRAW, RIDE, and SOLVE. Find out the steps that are cued by the letters of these four mnemonic strategies.

Part 4:
Learner Differences

Case 16: Include Me In

Emily Pendleton teaches fourth grade in a residential school in the Northeast. Her five students, three boys and two girls, have moderate to profound hearing losses. They all wear hearing aids and have speech skills at varying levels of intelligibility. Emily uses Simultaneous Communication for instructional purposes.

At the start of the second nine-week grading period, her principal, Trudie Lingold, stopped by to inform her that she would have a new student in her class. Rafael Garza, whose family recently moved from Mexico, has a mild, unilateral hearing loss. He wears a hearing aid and has fairly intelligible speech. According to the educational diagnosticians who were part of the intake team, he knows almost no English. One of the diagnosticians, Alexis Flores, who is fluent in Spanish, administered the *Dos Amigos Verbal Language Scales*, a screening tool that uses pairs of opposites in English and Spanish to determine functional language levels. Rafael recognized, pronounced, drew, or acted out examples of most of the words in Spanish. He identified only five of the English words. Alexis noted that these words were cognates of the Spanish equivalents, so he was probably making educated guesses. Nonetheless, he guessed right, a fact that allowed them to make the observation that he has competent reasoning skills.

During the collection of a written language sample, Rafael was shown a series of pictures of a boy ordering in a fast-food restaurant. When asked to attempt a narrative in English, he became visibly anxious and wrote two words: *He is*. He put down his pencil, looked at Alexis, and shrugged his shoulders. She gave him a fresh sheet of paper, handed him the pencil, and explained that he could now write in Spanish. His expression brightened as he took the pencil and proceeded to write a paragraph of six sentences in Spanish.

It All Depends

Emily asked Trudie Lingold if Rafael knew any sign language. He did not. He had been educated in an auditory/oral school in Mexico. He was very attuned to gestures, however, and had been able to communicate his needs to the staff. He also seemed to follow gestural communication easily. Trudie Lingold told Emily that the school's sign language coordinator had agreed to teach Rafael signs for 30 minutes after school each day. Moreover, it was anticipated that, by being in the dormitory, he would pick up new signs daily—and rapidly.

Trudie Lingold saw the anguish on Emily's face and encouraged her simply to do her best with Rafael, who would be showing up for class the following day. She explained to Emily that many of the second-language strategies she was already using with her current group of students would probably work equally well with Rafael. Emily smiled weakly and said that she would try hard to meet his academic needs just as she did with all of her students. As the principal was leaving, Emily found herself thinking this was easier said than done.

The following day in class, Rafael walked around to his classmates and shook their hands while nodding politely. Emily found this a gracious gesture, one that would endear him to his new classmates. After formally introducing Rafael to the class, Emily started the day with social studies. She had scheduled this class first so she could begin the day with a discussion of current events, the way she and her colleagues did every morning. One of her deaf colleagues who had attended a residential program had mentioned having a wonderful teacher who would always begin the day with the "Morning News." He said he and his classmates loved it because they began the day informed, just like hearing children who may have heard the same information from their parents' conversations or on TV.

After presenting a brief summary of current events, Emily went to the interactive whiteboard and touched a link she had preset. A map of Mexico appeared on the screen. When it dawned on Rafael what the image depicted, a smile lit up his face. Emily beckoned for Rafael to come forward and point out where he had lived in Mexico.

Case 16: INCLUDE ME IN

Excitedly, he came forward and did so. When he returned to his seat, she displayed a map of North America and, with her finger, traced the journey from Mexico to the United States. The students, even Rafael, seemed amazed at the great distance he and his family had traveled.

The content lessons went very smoothly. Emily regularly used visuals and manipulatives, and this approach seemed to help Rafael as well as her other students. A few times, he would even gesture and say something in Spanish, which she did not understand. She could only hope that her smiles and nods sufficiently conveyed that she acknowledged and appreciated his efforts to participate.

The last subject she taught was English language arts, a class in which Emily had anticipated Rafael would have the greatest trouble, especially in reading. The class began reading a story of a teen who gets into a motorcycle accident. Stopping at the point in the story immediately following the accident, she wrote the words *live* and *die* on the chalkboard, each word followed by a question mark. Then, she asked her students for a prediction regarding the young man's fate.

To her amazement, Rafael was the first student to raise his hand. He came to the whiteboard, picked up the green stylus, and placed a check mark next to the word *live*. He seemed so confident in his prediction that Emily responded with a puzzled expression and a shrug of her shoulders, which she hoped he would translate as, "How did you come to that conclusion?" Accurately interpreting her query, he grabbed the book from his desk, returned to the whiteboard, and selected the blue stylus. He looked intently at a page in the book, and copied this sentence: *He was revived by the paramedics.* Below the word *revived*, he wrote a Spanish word: *vivir*, to live. Then, with the red stylus, he drew a box around the letter *viv* in the words *revived* and *vivir*. Finally, he pointed at both boxes, nodded his head confidently, and returned to his desk, as if his actions had explained everything. In fact, they had. His inference was precisely on target. He had successfully used structural analysis based on similarities he observed between a familiar Spanish word and an unfamiliar English word to assist him with reading comprehension. Emily manifested her delight at Rafael's explanation with a radiant smile and a thumbs-up gesture.

It All Depends

After the class left, Emily knew she had to rethink her assumptions about Rafael. Perhaps teaching him would not be the enormously arduous task she had originally anticipated. It was clear to her that he was an intelligent, motivated boy who brought a lot to the table. She still felt uncertainty. How was she going to figure out the full range of Rafael's strengths and use them to teach him required fourth-grade academic content while developing his English proficiency?

QUESTIONS FOR REFLECTION

1. What are the key issues presented in this case?
2. In what ways are Rafael's learning challenges in his present educational setting similar to—and different from—those of his deaf classmates who have been learning English?
3. What strengths does Rafael exhibit that can be capitalized on to enable academic success in his current educational environment?
4. What is your assessment of Emily's efforts to accommodate Rafael on his first day as a student in her classroom?
5. What strategies can Emily use to facilitate Rafael's academic achievement in her class?
6. What strategies can Emily use to facilitate interaction between Rafael and his classmates when working in pairs or groups until his English and sign language skills improve?

EXTENSION ACTIVITIES

1. Identify print and Internet sources with information and activities for students whose first language is not English.
2. Identify print and Internet resources with information on culturally diverse deaf individuals.
3. Contact several teachers of the deaf, and ask them to identify ways that they address the needs of culturally diverse students in their classrooms.

4. Contact a staff development director, and find out what types of inservice activities are provided to help teachers more effectively work with culturally diverse students and their families.
5. Examine your own teacher education program. How are you being prepared to deliver culturally responsive instruction to (a) deaf students from various racial and ethnic backgrounds and (b) deaf students who may have grown up with a primary spoken language other than English?

Case 17: Things Just Don't Add Up

Joanna Katz is a first-year itinerant teacher whose caseload includes 14 deaf students in four schools in the Northwest. Joanna is deaf, with a moderate hearing loss in both ears. She wears in-the-ear hearing aids, and her speech is generally intelligible. By reason of deafness in her family, sign language was a part of the communication repertoire in her home as she grew up.

Because of her own hearing loss and personal experiences with classroom accommodations, Joanna is highly motivated to troubleshoot the challenges involved in meeting the needs of the deaf and hard of hearing students in her school district. Another source of motivation for Joanna is that no two days—or students—are alike, and the situations about which she is asked to consult challenge her knowledge and creativity to their limits. Her current challenge is third grader Austin Bradley, who will become a direct-serve student in a couple of days. Austin has a severe hearing loss, communicates in sign language, and has been successfully mainstreamed since kindergarten. According to his teacher, Olivia Caffrey, Austin is performing well in every subject area except mathematics.

Although Austin has never failed mathematics, it has always been his worst subject. His grades in mathematics don't match his grades in other subject areas or his potential. Because of the seeming discrepancy between his mathematics performance and his overall intelligence, his teachers feel there is a strong possibility he has a learning disability that specifically affects his ability to do mathematics. His parents report that at home, he cannot perform basic mathematical applications the way they feel he should be able to do. They have authorized Joanna do whatever assessment is necessary to diagnose Austin's problems.

Joanna met with Edwin Tifford, the district psychologist, who provided her with a screening checklist for *dyscalculia*, a disorder that affects an individual's ability to do mathematics. The checklist, completed by teacher Olivia Caffrey, indicated that Austin displayed many of the characteristics indicative of dyscalculia. Edwin Tifford said that, based on his review of Austin's cumulative folder, an interview with Austin, parental observations, and the results of the screening checklist, Austin's math difficulties were severe enough to meet the criteria of dyscalculia. His professional opinion was that Austin needed intervention beyond the mathematics instruction he was receiving.

Joanna said that she would be the person providing tutoring for Austin and requested guidance on how to proceed. First, Mr. Tifford suggested that she examine any specific error patterns on worksheets done in class so that her intervention would be situation-specific and therefore more useful. He remarked that there was almost always a method that students used to arrive at even wrong answers. Second, he recommended that she focus on the problem characteristics that Olivia Caffrey identified as "frequent" on the screening checklist. He encouraged Joanna to contact him again if she did not observe any progress in Austin after a few weeks. She thanked him for his assistance.

Joanna reviewed Austin's daily schedule. All third graders had a computer class at some point in each day, during which time their teachers had a planning period. She arranged that Austin would attend the computer class twice a week and, the other three days, Joanna would tutor him in mathematics during that same period. Austin was eager to improve his mathematics grades, and he and his parents readily agreed to the schedule adjustment. Joanna contacted the principal at Austin's school to find a location conducive to providing the tutoring sessions.

During a break, Joanna took a look at the areas from the screening checklist Edwin Tifford had suggested she address, the ones Olivia Caffrey had indicated occurred with frequency.

Case 17: THINGS JUST DON'T ADD UP

- *Lack of estimation skills*
- *Problems recognizing patterns*
- *Problems visualizing math concepts nonverbally*
- *Inability to perform basic operations*
- *Misaligns written numerals on paper*
- *Difficulty generalizing mathematics to real life*
- *Lacks ability to reason mathematically*
- *Approaches solving word problems unsystematically*
- *Experiences math anxiety and aviodance*
- *Does not know if an answer to a math problem is logical*

Joanna realized she needed some time to research strategies to address these issues. For the first tutoring session, she wanted to work on a short-term goal so that Austin could experience some immediate success. Austin's class recently had been introduced to the process of multiplying one-digit numbers by two-digit numbers with regrouping. His teacher provided Joanna with five problems Austin had attempted to solve. All of his answers were incorrect. Although the situation looked bleak, Joanna recalled the psychologist's statement that students' mathematics errors were rarely random.

Joanna reviewed Austin's mathematics worksheet again. The first time she glanced at it, she saw no rhyme or reason to Austin's thought processes. However, she urgently needed to make some discovery soon, because their first session was scheduled for the next morning, and she wanted to be ready with a solid idea of his specific problem and to target remedial instruction she could provide.

1	2	3	1	2
13	34	57	49	28
x 4	x 6	x 5	x 2	x 3
82	304	405	108	124

How was he attempting to solve these problems? Joanna wondered to herself.

It All Depends

Questions for Reflection

1. What are the key issues presented in this case?
2. What error pattern should Joanna be able to identify in Austin's mathematics sample? What are ways she might remediate this problem?
3. What are suggestions for teachers who have a dyscalculic student in a self-contained setting, without access to an identified professional on staff to provide additional instruction?
4. What is your assessment of the referral and identification process in this case?

Extension Activities

1. Choose three of the characteristics indicated as frequent problems for Austin, and identify two strategies for remediating the problem. Use print, Internet, or human resources to assist you in this task.
2. Contact several teachers of the deaf. Ask them:
   - What common learning disabilities do their students exhibit, what are the characteristics of the learning disabilities, and what interventions do they use to help the students overcome or compensate for their learning disorders?
   - What is the referral process for initiating a request for a formal assessment to diagnose students experiencing extreme academic, behavior, and social problems and to lend assistance and resources beyond those that teachers have been able to provide in the classroom setting?
3. Identify four Internet sources that specialize in information and resources for helping students with various types of learning disabilities.

Case 18: Disorderly Conduct

Angela Hutchins is a first-year resource teacher in a middle school. The eight students for whom she is responsible include four students with severe to profound hearing losses. With an educational interpreter, they take their content courses in the general education classroom. In the resource room, Angela teaches these four students the English language arts curriculum standards. The other four students have slight to mild hearing losses and are fully mainstreamed. Angela consults with all of the general education teachers on a regular basis.

Two weeks after the new school year started, the classes for the deaf and hard of hearing students were going well, for the most part. Students had settled in and become comfortable with their new teachers and new learning environments. This was the case for all of the students except one: Thad Fletcher.

Thad is a sixth grader, and this is his first experience in a mainstream setting. From kindergarten through fifth grade, he attended an oral day school program, in which he consistently made As and Bs. In light of his strong academic foundation, his parents felt the time was right to place him in a setting in which he could continue to develop academically while having the opportunity to interact with hearing peers.

Since age three, Thad has had a cochlear implant, which resulted in significant gains in his sound awareness and speech understanding. He hears vowel sounds and most consonant sounds clearly, occasionally missing unvoiced consonant sounds. He has only mild speech problems, and he is generally understood when he speaks. On paper, his speech, auditory, and academic skills suggest that he is a good candidate for inclusion into general education classes. His relative weakness is in the area of English language arts. His reading level is a year below grade-level expectation, and his written language,

It All Depends

while comprehensible, has minor deficits that need refinement. Accordingly, the multidisciplinary team (MDT) decided that, for this academic year, Thad would receive direct services in English language arts from Angela in the resource room setting, while being mainstreamed into the general education classroom for his content area courses and physical education.

Angela met with Thad's teachers and provided tips on communication, visual presentation strategies, and instructional accommodations. Initially, his teachers were excited about the challenge of teaching a student with a hearing loss. Unfortunately, this favorable sentiment did not last very long. Thad's behavior in class quickly became so problematic that the principal, Pierre Norris, asked Angela to gather data and draft a behavioral intervention plan (BIP) that could be presented to the MDT as a starting point for addressing Thad's unacceptable behavior. Angela was not unfamiliar with Thad's problems. Sometimes when he showed up for English language arts, he would be agitated. He would usually say that he was upset because students were teasing him—about his speech, his implant, his occasional misunderstanding when they or the teacher spoke. One day, however, he had become so furious that it took both Angela and the guidance counselor to calm him down and remove him from one of his mainstreamed classes.

It took Angela a few days to find convenient times to meet with Thad's teachers. On Friday morning, she completed the last of the teacher interviews. What she needed to do next was review the data she had collected and translate this information into a workable BIP. She knew this would be a challenging task, but her college behavior management course had been one of her favorites, and she looked forward to putting the principles she had learned into action. She began the process of reviewing her notes.

Thad's teachers state that he often disrupts their classes. His statements indicate that he feels that students are always making fun of him. When he answered a question wrong in social studies class, a boy sitting next to him looked in his direction, and Thad shook his fist angrily at the boy. The teacher saw no evidence that Thad was being insulted, only that the boy, as well as other students, was looking in his direction. In mathematics class, while Thad

Case 18: DISORDERLY CONDUCT

was working a problem at the chalkboard, he had a decimal in the wrong place in his answer. When a classmate pointed out this mistake, he became visibly anxious and threw the chalk he had been writing with in her direction. If she had not leaned quickly to her right, it would have struck her.

In his science class, when they were talking about examples of magnets, a student asked Thad if part of his implant was held in place by a magnet. The question appeared to be legitimate, not asked in a derisive manner. However, Thad became enraged, threw his textbook at the boy, yelled an obscenity at him, pushed over his own desk, and stormed out of the classroom. His physical education teacher said that Thad's clashes with other students were happening with increasing frequency and intensity. In fact, if there was an apparatus other than a ball involved in a sports activity, she would not allow Thad to participate, because of the great likelihood that his negative behavior might include hitting another student with a bat or a racquet. She said, while this might seem extreme, she has the welfare and safety of the other students to consider.

After perusing her notes, Angela was saddened. The portrait of Thad that had been painted was drastically different from the boy she worked with in her resource room, the boy who was smart, respectful, and loved computers and drawing. Admittedly, she worked with him primarily one-on-one or when other deaf and hard of hearing students were in the resource room. Once in a while, if Thad and another student were working on the same skill, she would have them work together on activities such as paired guided reading and learning partner journals. In the resource room, he had never exhibited any disruptive behavior.

Thad's parents, with whom she talked by telephone, stated that Thad got along splendidly with his sister and brothers. They have never witnessed the tempestuous, volatile behavior described by his teachers.

Thad's parents questioned their decision to place their son in an inclusive setting, because one of the intended outcomes, learning to interact with his hearing peers, was obviously not occurring. Angela reminded them that they had made a decision they felt was in the best interest of their son. She assured them that she and other school personnel were going to develop a plan that would teach Thad self-discipline and conflict resolution skills that would help him

It All Depends

to decrease disruptive behaviors and learn appropriate social interaction skills.

Angela encouraged the Fletchers to discuss Thad's behavior problems with him that weekend. She told them that the school would attempt to resolve his issues as soon as possible and said the principal would like them to meet as part of the MDT to discuss and finalize a BIP on Monday morning at 8:00. The parents affirmed that one or both of them would definitely be present. After her conversation with the Fletchers, she informed principal Pierre Norris that one or both parents would be in attendance. He said he would let the other team members know about the meeting.

The principal said he was aware that this was the first BIP Angela would be drafting and discussing, but he was confident that she would do a commendable job. He reminded her to address all of the necessary components: (1) targeted problem behavior, (2) desired replacement behavior, (3) methods of teaching the replacement behavior, (4) methods of measuring progress, (5) positive consequences for displaying the replacement behavior, (6) negative consequences for displaying inappropriate behavior, and (7) accommodations to assist the student in displaying the replacement behavior. She assured him that she would. Then, she packed up for the day and walked to her car, looking forward to a productive weekend of completing lots of little projects around the house and one major project: getting Thad's derailed school experience back on track.

QUESTIONS FOR REFLECTION

1. What are the key issues presented in this case?
2. What are some ways that Angela can address each of the required components of the BIP for Thad?
3. A functional behavior assessment (FBA) is developed as a precursor to a BIP to gather information needed to write a meaningful, relevant support plan. Three typical FBA questions are listed on the following page. With regard to Thad's situation, how would you answer them?

Case 18: DISORDERLY CONDUCT

- What is your hypothesis about the function or purpose that Thad's misbehavior serves for him?
- Under what circumstances is Thad's misbehavior most likely to occur?
- Under what circumstances is Thad's misbehavior least likely to occur?

Extension Activities

1. When students have frequent conflicts with others, they need to not only learn to control their antisocial behavior but also to develop appropriate social skills. Identify social skills curricula and materials designed to assist students who are deficient in social competencies.
2. Identify five behavior rating scales used to evaluate the conduct of students who exhibit inappropriate behavior.
3. Rating scales measure student behavior indirectly. However, direct observations allow for firsthand documentation of actual behavior as it occurs in a particular setting. Identify four procedures for conducting systematic direct observations of students, and explain what each procedure entails.
4. During a field experience, use one of the observation procedures identified in the previous item to collect data on actual students. It is preferable that you ask the teacher to identify students who have demonstrated problematic behaviors that he or she would like documented. Doing so will make this process a more credible and useful activity.

Case 19: Spoiled for Choice

As a first-year teacher, Gage McNair was on pins and needles in anticipation of his third observation during the first quarter of the school year. Anxious feelings aside, in reality, he felt fortunate to have landed his dream job of teaching fifth graders in a Total Communication (TC) day school. Feeling comfortable signing and speaking together, he had performed well in his Simultaneous Communication courses in college. Moreover, he had always wanted to teach fifth graders, because there was a deep sense of responsibility on their teachers' part to prepare students not only with grade-level information but also with skills that would enable them to transition smoothly from elementary school to secondary school.

Today, he was being observed teaching a social studies lesson by the Hearing Impairment Teacher Coordinator, Yuna Hirano. The additional pressure he felt derived from the fact that Ms. Hirano had double majored in Deaf Education and Social Studies, so her knowledge of the content, as well as her knowledge of teaching deaf students, was at the highest level. After their first observation, she had indicated that by observing the same subject multiple times, she would be able to better evaluate his lesson delivery and provide a more valid observation. He agreed, thinking that her rationale made sense, because she would be comparing apples and apples, so to speak.

On the day of the observation, Gage had planned a lesson on the following objective within the civics strand of the state-mandated social studies curriculum: *describe the organizational structure and powers of the federal government*. To maintain consistency in the approach to all of his instruction, he followed a strict concept teaching model: defining terms, stating examples, providing nonexamples, and testing for attainment. Ironically, it turned out to be the rigid adherence to this process that was main concern raised in the post-observation conference.

It All Depends

Gage's mood brightened when Ms. Hirano began her feedback by applauding his organizational skills. She added that his objectives were aligned with the fifth-grade state standards for social studies, and that he consistently developed thoughtful lesson plans, implementing them with fidelity. At this juncture, Gage tensed up, certain that a "but" was forthcoming. He was right. She pointed out that, although the students were attentive, they did not seem truly engaged. She said that they passively received the information presented and answered questions when posed. She suggested that a more active learning approach, one that ramped up the level of student motivation, would be helpful. He quickly asserted that he was following what he had learned was an accepted model for teaching concepts.

Ms. Hirano promptly reassured Gage that he was not doing anything that was inappropriate. However, she stated that his teaching approach was identical to his instruction of lessons during the past two observations. She emphasized that what his teaching lacked was not insufficient planning but rather insufficient variety, which could be built into any phase of a concept lesson. For instance, she explained that, when providing examples, students could do a think-pair-share and offer additional examples that applied. Furthermore, if concepts lend themselves to visual displays, students could pair up and draw examples of them or even act them out. By doing so, he would capitalize on three additional intelligences: interpersonal, visual-spatial, and bodily-kinesthetic. Accordingly, variety could be provided without sacrificing the instructional syntax of the concept teaching model.

Having gained more clarity about building variety into his lessons, Gage said, "I recall learning about the multiple intelligences in my educational psychology course."

After tapping her right temple, as if to dislodge a stubborn idea, Ms. Hirano suddenly snapped her fingers and said exuberantly, "I have the perfect strategy for you to try. At the end of the next lesson I observe, I want you to provide your students with a choice board of activities to extend their understanding of the lesson concept and aid in transferring it to long-term memory, which I'm sure you also learned about in that educational psychology course."

Case 19: SPOILED FOR CHOICE

Confidently, Gage replied, "I did." Hesitantly, he continued, "But what's a choice board?"

She explained, "In a nutshell, it is a type of learning menu that provides an array of activities from which students can choose to demonstrate their learning. A common format is a tic-tac-toe table. In the cells of the table, the teacher identifies a variety of learning activities."

"OK, I understand the format," he said, "but how can I make sure that the tasks are ~~really~~ decidedly different from each other?"

"Excellent question," she replied. "That's where the intelligences come into play. Differentiation can be achieved in a number of ways, but teachers will often create activities based on each of the multiple intelligences and require that students complete two or more of the activities. There are other formats, but the one I have described is a simple way to differentiate instruction for your students. Sure, hearing loss inclines them to learn primarily through a visual orientation. However, there are other modalities and pathways for them to acquire and demonstrate knowledge."

"I'm already thinking of ideas," Gage said excitedly. "And I know the students will be more involved and more motivated. Thanks so much for your feedback and guidance. Next time, I guarantee you will see a difference in the level of student involvement throughout the lesson."

"Giving students choices will increase their motivation," Ms. Hirano said. Then, she quickly added, "And that is a principle you should have learned—"

Recognizing where Ms. Hirano was going with her statement, Gage chuckled and jumped in to finish her sentence, "I know, I know—in my educational psychology course."

It All Depends

QUESTIONS FOR REFLECTION

1. What are the key issues presented in this case?
2. Two words that came up in the case are consistency and variety, which are antithetical concepts. How do you think that teachers can achieve a balance between the two concepts when planning for instruction?
3. What is a fundamental problem with Gage's overall approach to instructional planning?
4. In Gage's choice board for the learning outcome *describe the organizational structure and powers of the federal government*, identify learning experiences he could provide his students consistent with these four intelligences:
   - interpersonal
   - visual-spatial
   - verbal-linguistic
   - bodily-kinesthetic

EXTENSION ACTIVITIES

1. Find out the difference between the two basic types of concept instruction: concept teaching and concept attainment.
2. Summarize the principles of three theories of motivation.
3. A choice board is only one example of a learning menu. Locate two other examples of learning menus, and describe how to create them.

Case 20: Same Difference

Rustin Bridgewater was energized at the prospect of starting his first professional job. He had searched online and found an opening at a residential program for a secondary Transition Education teacher for seniors with special needs. The position caught his eye because, in his teacher education program, he had been taught about transition in his career education course and was extremely interested in the topic. Also, in his field experiences, he had derived the greatest satisfaction when working with students who struggled with learning. In this setting, he theorized, any potential challenges would be overbalanced by the high motivation levels of the students, who would be learning concepts and skills directly applicable to independent living and the world of work that most would be pursuing soon after graduation.

Shortly after getting the job, Rustin had an opportunity to meet with Lanette Vaughn, the supervisor of the school's secondary program. She explained that all of the students he would be teaching were identified as having an intellectual disability in addition to their deafness. Accordingly, they were not required to take the statewide competency assessment, because they would not be following the statewide general curriculum. She added that, alternatively, the students were expected to meet the objectives of a standards-based individualized education program (IEP). Upon graduation, the students would receive an IEP diploma. She emphasized that even though the state department of education allowed districts to set their own specific requirements for these students, there is a firm state guideline that the IEP goals—in essence, the curriculum for special needs students—must derive from the general curriculum standards.

Realizing that the summer months would pass in the blink of an eye, Rustin asked Ms. Vaughn to provide more direction that

It All Depends

would help him to prepare for the fall. That way, he would be able to use his time most effectively. She explained that because the students were in a self-contained setting, he would be teaching them the four core subjects: math, science, social studies, and English language arts. She suggested that it would be prudent for him to review the standards in those subject areas and select or adapt benchmarks that would best enable the students to be good employees and, more important, productive citizens. These benchmarks would constitute his students' curriculum. Before concluding the meeting, Rustin had a brainstorm: using social studies as the centerpiece of the curriculum, because this subject included civics and economics, topics of particular importance to young adults on the verge of graduation. When he shared his thoughts with Ms. Vaughn, she smiled and nodded approvingly. Pleased that he had a workable tentative plan, he thanked her for her assistance and made his exit.

After the meeting, Rustin drove back to the motel where he was staying for a few days as he familiarized himself with the city and searched for an apartment. Although he had planned to look at the classifieds for a place to rent, he gave in to a more pressing desire to go online and review the state curriculum standards. He decided to spend a short period of time examining the social studies curriculum since it would be the nucleus of the overall curriculum. He clicked on the civics strand. The first benchmark stated that *students will explain how laws safeguard individual rights.* Perfect, he thought. He could shape this learning outcome into a focus on the students' rights under the Americans with Disabilities Act (ADA). Next, he accessed the economics strand. One of the benchmarks indicated that students will *determine how earnings of workers are determined.* No adaptation needed, he thought. It was relevant to his students, as stated. Moreover, he could integrate math content. As he viewed other benchmarks, he jotted down notes, elated as he watched the alternative curriculum take shape before his very eyes.

After a few hours, Rustin logged off the department of education site, feeling a sense of confidence with the educational direction he had decided to pursue. Rather than being apprehensive about the task, he had to admit that he was enjoying the task of customizing

Case 20: SAME DIFFERENCE

the curriculum he would be using. This process reminded him of one of his college courses, Curriculum and Instruction, the *what* and *how* of teaching, respectively. He felt comfortable with what students would be learning. Now, he had to concern himself with how he would teach them. What would be the most effective instructional techniques for maximizing the learning of deaf students with intellectual disabilities? His senior seminar had briefly touched on the nature and needs of deaf students with additional disabilities. He remembered Professor Dyson emphasizing that the condition of deafness is substantially more complex for students when it interacts with other disabilities. He was pretty certain that he had kept his notes from that course. He knew he would be able to find them in the prodigious amount of college paperwork he had decided he might need one day. Reality check, he thought: One of those days was here.

QUESTIONS FOR REFLECTION

1. What are the key issues presented in this case?
2. For students following an alternative curriculum, what variables should go into the decision-making process regarding the most appropriate curriculum objectives for them? How might these variables differ for elementary and secondary students?
3. All students with disabilities must have transition goals included in their IEPs no later than age 16. How might these goals be similar and different for deaf students in a standard-diploma track and those in an alternative-diploma track?

EXTENSION ACTIVITIES

1. Diploma options for students with disabilities vary among the states. Find out the diploma options for students with disabilities in the state in which you hope to teach. If you have no preference, select the state in which you will receive your initial teacher certification.

It All Depends

2. Find out the percentage of deaf students estimated to have additional disabilities. Specify the percentage of students in the various disability categories.
3. Identify instructional strategies for students with intellectual disabilities that can complement strategies for accommodating the learning needs of typical deaf and hard of hearing students.

Part 5:
Educational Planning

Case 21: A Valuable Lesson

Ashlyn Tapley is a first-year teacher of third graders in a self-contained classroom at a public school. She teaches six students with a continuum of hearing loss ranging from severe to profound. She feels that, so far, she has been doing a satisfactory job as a classroom teacher. However, although her students seem to master basic academic facts and rules, they have difficulty applying them. They also tend to have gaps in their learning and, frequently, she finds herself having to go back and reteach information she assumed they already had acquired. The bottom line is that she definitely thinks her students could be learning more effectively. Therefore, she was hoping to get some useful feedback from Patrick McGuire, the district's Support Services Specialist for the Deaf & Hard of Hearing Program, who was coming one day soon to do his first classroom observation of her instruction.

Ashlyn planned to teach her students how to formulate yes/no questions that day. She didn't anticipate any problems, because inverting the subject and verb in a sentence is pretty straightforward. So she did not feel the need to spend much of her planning time researching the concept itself. Rather, she decided she would spend her time more prudently coming up with interesting example sentences that would appeal to the students. She was certain she would get high marks on creativity. Also, she planned to demonstrate the process of converting declarative sentences to yes/no questions, use arrows to make the process visual, and have the students pair off and write two sentences: a declarative sentence and its corresponding yes/no question. She felt confident because she had planned a good lesson, one that included demonstration, a visual strategy, and cooperative learning.

Patrick McGuire appeared a few minutes before the English language arts lesson was to begin. Ashlyn introduced him, explained

It All Depends

why he was there, and the students greeted him graciously. After he moved to the back of the classroom and took a seat, Ashlyn began the lesson, closely adhering to the script she had planned. She started by explaining the objective and why it was important to learn the skill, and proceeded to explain the inversion process involved, also indicating capitalization and punctuation changes that were necessary. Next, she demonstrated by writing two examples on the chalkboard. The first sentence was *Harry Potter is a boy*. She drew arrows above and below the subject and verb to show they should be reversed. Then, she wrote *Is Harry Potter a boy?* Her second sentence was *The students are smart*. A student, Allan, raised his hand and volunteered to make the statement a question. Pleased with his initiative, she held out the chalk. Allan imitated what she had done with the previous example and produced the question *Are the students smart?* She said that Allan's correct question proved that her students are very smart, a remark that was followed by laughter from the class.

At this point, Ashlyn's apprehension about being observed subsided, and she felt that she could finally relax. She asked students who did not understand the lesson to raise their hands. Since no one did, she continued with the next phase of her lesson. She divided the students into pairs and gave each student a strip of poster board. She explained that they would write a statement on one strip and the corresponding yes/no question on the other one. Then, they would come forward and place the two sentences in the pocket chart she had attached to the chalkboard.

Ten minutes later, the students signaled that they had finished the task. Tammy and Marcus came forward and displayed their sentences:

| Marcus is tall. | Is Marcus tall? |

Ashlyn praised them for a job well done. Their bright smiles conveyed the pride of accomplishment. Next, she summoned Allan and Marissa. They placed their sentences into the chart pockets and read them:

Case 21: A VALUABLE LESSON

> They like school.

> Like they school?

Ashlyn explained that their second sentence was not an acceptable question. Allan and Marissa looked at her quizzically. Then, Allan placed his right index finger over the word *like* and traced it in an arc over and in front of the word *they*, indicating that they had done what they had seen in her demonstration. Ashlyn's heart sank. Her face registered dismay, and she did not know exactly what to do in this situation. So she said she would explain more later and quickly motioned for the final pair, Craig and Elijah, to present. Ashlyn emitted a heavy sigh as she viewed the sentences:

> Students ride the school bus.

> Ride students the school bus?

She was acutely aware that her lesson was going downhill fast. Bewildered, she chose not to comment on the accuracy of the question, deciding instead to simply thank the pair for working together so well. Fortunately, the class period was over, and the educational interpreter, Chloe Bradley, arrived to accompany the students to their art class.

In the post-observation conference, Patrick McGuire started by asking Ashlyn how she felt about the lesson. She stated that she felt good about the actual instructional process, but honestly conceded that she had, obviously, not fully considered all aspects of the skill she had attempted to teach. McGuire agreed and suggested that the skill she was trying to teach as a single lesson was more appropriately a unit topic that incorporated multiple lessons. He encouraged her to do a task analysis for future skills and concepts, regardless of how simple they might appear to be. He pointed out that new teachers often teach from the perspective of *their* knowledge base rather than from the perspective of a novice learner.

It All Depends

Patrick McGuire further stated that some deaf students might not have the subskills necessary to master larger, more encompassing skills, or they may lack the background knowledge to understand larger concepts. As an example, he shared with her an observation he had done the previous year with a new teacher of the deaf who taught first graders. This beginning teacher had taught personal pronouns, finally giving his students an exercise he had taken from a workbook. The students did poorly. After debriefing by interviewing the students, they found that the students actually understood the lesson. The reason they had not done well on the worksheet was that they didn't recognize whether many of the names represented males or females, so many of the pronouns they selected were incorrect. The distinction between male and female names was not a possible area of confusion the teacher had taken into consideration when planning. He said it had never crossed his mind. However, it was obviously knowledge that was necessary for students to possess in order to successfully complete the worksheet.

Ashlyn laughed and said she could identify with this teacher, prompting McGuire to return to his original advice. He emphasized that a task analysis or a concept analysis allows the teacher to ensure that students have required background knowledge or to teach it, if necessary, to increase the likelihood that students will master content and language lesson objectives. Ashlyn stated that she had learned about doing a task analysis in her teacher education program and certainly saw the wisdom of putting time and effort into analyzing lesson *content* as well as determining lesson *procedures*, acknowledging that, for her yes/no question lesson, her planning focus had been primarily on the latter.

Ashlyn assured Mr. McGuire that, from now on, she would identify the enabling skills her students needed for learning the objectives she planned to teach. He nodded reassuringly and told her not to despair, that even veteran teachers, on occasion, get up to teach a lesson and realize they had not covered all the bases when planning. He explained that such situations are not irrevocable. He directed her to e-mail him the subskills she had identified. He stated

Case 21: A VALUABLE LESSON

that he checked his e-mail regularly and would offer her feedback on her efforts. She thanked him for his support, and he rose to leave.

When the door closed, Ashlyn took several deep breaths, walked slowly to her desk, eased into her chair, and put her head in her hands. Before she had time to feel too sorry for herself, however, the door opened, and six lively children besieged her, showing her an art project they had completed. Sharing in their educational successes buoyed her spirits and, as she placed manipulatives on the front table for a mathematics lesson, this sentiment fueled her resolve to make sure that she helped them successfully learn not only the ins and outs of writing yes/no questions but also every other standard in the third-grade curriculum that she was expected to teach them.

Questions for Reflection

1. What are the key issues presented in the case?
2. What is your general assessment of Ashlyn as a beginning teacher?
3. Ashlyn indicated that in her teacher education program, she learned about doing a task analysis as part of planning to teach a skill. What might be a reason or reasons that Ashlyn did not apply this knowledge?
4. Considering the skill that Ashlyn was endeavoring to teach, what are some subskills that she needs to consider addressing, possibly as mini-lessons or full-fledged lessons?
5. What are some strengths of the lesson that Ashlyn taught?
6. How would you assess the way in which Ashlyn handled the pairs that displayed ungrammatical questions?
7. As Patrick McGuire stated, even with careful planning, teachers might experience instances when they make mistakes in the course of delivering instruction. How might a teacher handle these awkward times?

It All Depends

Extension Activities

1. A *task analysis* identifies the specific behaviors (mental and/or physical) involved in performing a skill. Access the curriculum standards for the state in which your teacher education program is located or one in which you plan to seek employment upon graduation. Identify two skills that students are expected to demonstrate, and do a task analysis for each skill.
2. In addition to skills in the curriculum, there are many concepts that students are expected to learn. Preparation for teaching concepts can involve two planning tools. The first is a *concept map* (sometimes called a *concept hierarchy*), which identifies a <u>superordinate</u> concept (the larger category to which the concept belongs), <u>coordinate</u> concepts (other subsets of the superordinate concept), and <u>subordinate</u> concepts (subsets of the concept being taught). The second is a *concept analysis*, which describes a concept, including its definition, characteristics, examples, and nonexamples. In the curriculum frameworks you accessed, identify two concepts and do both a concept map and a concept analysis for each one.

Case 22: The Ultimate Goal

Damon Brooks is a first-year teacher at a residential school in the Midwest. He teaches seven fourth graders with severe to profound hearing losses, four boys and three girls, all of whom are motivated and eager to learn. He enjoys coming up with inventive ways to deliver instruction to this capable group of children. Since the school year began, he has discovered a number of strategies that work well with this group. Damon feels an enormous sense of pride when he turns in his lesson plans to the principal, Janet Young. On several occasions, she has commended him on his lesson plans.

She stopped by his classroom yesterday to observe a lesson she said looked especially interesting on paper. Before leaving, she praised him and commented that he seemed keenly aware of specific instructional supports the students needed to learn the benchmarks in the state curriculum. She added that this ability would serve him well when he began writing IEPs for his students, pointing out that Brenda Rothstein, the school's IEP coordinator, would be contacting him later in the day to set up a time to discuss this important process.

During his planning time, his computer alerted him that he had an e-mail message. It was from Brenda Rothstein, who wanted to meet with him after the students left for the day. He replied that he would be available. When the last student walked out the door, he quickly went online to access the state's *IEP Writing Guide*, because he wanted to appear somewhat knowledgeable about the process. He did not get far in skimming the document before he heard the door open and turned to see Brenda Rothstein enter. She briefly reviewed the basic IEP components, stating that Damon's primary role would be writing goals that would enable his students' participation in the general curriculum. Damon indicated that he felt he had a fair idea about how to do this.

It All Depends

They decided to discuss one student in detail. Then, during the week, Damon could write some IEP goals and objectives, which Brenda Rothstein could review next week and offer some feedback. Damon agreed with this idea and suggested discussing Brandon Ashby, the only one of his seven students who had not started at the residential school as a kindergartener. She nodded her consent.

Damon began. Brandon Ashby is 11 years old and profoundly deaf. He has been deaf since birth. Brandon uses ASL to communicate, as do his parents, who are both deaf. Until this academic year, Brandon attended a public school, where he was mainstreamed with hearing students in every class except English language arts. He spent this time in a resource room with a certified teacher of the deaf. His parents placed him in a public school program so that he could feel comfortable interacting with children who could hear. Over the years, he has failed to interact significantly with his hearing classmates and has not made any friends. Also, for the past couple of years, his grades have been in decline. So his parents decided to send him to the state's residential school where, they hoped, their son would make friends and achieve better grades.

Even at the residential school, Brandon has failed to make friends. He is hesitant to approach his classmates and become involved in activities. He never initiates greetings and, even when his peers sign "Good morning," Brandon disregards them, goes directly to his desk, and sits down. This reluctance is also problematic when there are cooperative learning assignments, because he does not interact and contribute his ideas. Brandon's parents have expressed their concern, because socialization opportunities were a major reason they decided to send their son to this school.

Brandon enjoys science and social studies. He acquires basic facts easily but often has difficulty identifying relationships between those facts. This problem impedes him from processing information at higher levels such as comparing and contrasting concepts. His reading level, according to the *Woodcock Reading Mastery Test*, is 3.0. It may, in fact, be higher, but Brandon doesn't seem to know how to respond to different types of questions. On teacher-made tests, he answers yes/no questions fine, but he has more difficulty with

Case 22: THE ULTIMATE GOAL

answering "wh" questions. On a social studies test, one item asked: When did the Civil War begin? Brandon wrote: *North states fought South states*, an answer signifying that he understood the content but responded inappropriately.

TOWL (Test of Written Language) results indicate that Brandon's grammar, syntax, and spelling are good. However, they also indicate that his writing tends to be short and choppy. He includes main ideas but does not elaborate with more than one or two sentences. In mathematics, Brandon does basic computations satisfactorily. However, his skills break down with word problems that require application of these skills.

Brandon's grades don't really reflect his true abilities. Sometimes, when information is being presented, he doesn't consistently pay attention. When he is redirected, he is never oppositional and always complies. Even when he is doing independent seatwork and tests, he seems to be distracted. Thus when he makes a low grade, it is more often than not a result of partially completed work rather than lack of knowledge.

Overall, Damon concluded, it was his opinion that Brandon is an intelligent, capable student with a lot of untapped ability. Brenda Rothstein encouraged Damon to remember that assessment of Brandon, because the purpose of IEP goals is to help students realize their full potential. They shook hands and confirmed next week's meeting.

Damon sat at his computer and decided to write a couple of IEP goals before going home. While his description of Brandon had seemed to flow effortlessly, he could not seem to activate his brain cells, and he simply sat staring bleakly at the monitor.

Glancing at the time in the lower right corner of the screen, he decided to take off when, after five minutes, the document remained blank.

It All Depends

QUESTIONS FOR REFLECTION

1. What are the key issues presented in this case?
2. Based on Damon's narrative as a solid source of information, what are four measurable annual goals that could be written for Brandon? (Note: Make sure that the goals are measurable so that monitoring and measuring progress is possible.)
3. How might the information contained in Damon's narrative be helpful in contributing to components of the IEP other than the writing of annual goals?

EXTENSION ACTIVITIES

1. Access the U.S. Department of Education's publication *A Guide to the Individualized Education Program* at www.ed.gov/parents/needs/speced/iepguide/index.html. Find out what components, in addition to annual goals, should comprise the IEP.
2. Take a look at IEPs written by several practicing teachers. Note how the information satisfies the federally mandated components of the document.
3. See if you can sit in on an IEP conference to observe firsthand how IEP goals are presented and discussed.

Case 23: A Smooth Transition

Claire O'Connor is enjoying her first year as an itinerant teacher in a small town in the Southwest. Though her caseload is small, it presents more than its fair share of challenges, because she serves 15 students K–12. The variety is appealing in that it allows her to use all of the skills she learned in her undergraduate program. She has to use her knowledge of development of younger and older students, language arts, content subjects, speech, amplification, sign language, and cultural diversity.

Two weeks ago, Claire participated on the multidisciplinary team (MDT) to develop IEPs, the first one she has contributed to since beginning her job. She found this process extremely gratifying. So often, she is alone in her car or working one-on-one tutoring students or consulting with teachers. These spring IEP conferences have given her the opportunity to work as part of a group, an educational team. Also, she enjoyed collecting data from teachers, identifying students' weaknesses, and writing corresponding goals to mitigate the deficiencies and increase learning.

The next IEP conference would involve a different component. The Director of Exceptional Student Services, Isaac Reid, informed her that this IEP would be for a junior: Nita Carson, a 17-year-old student. Therefore, Claire would need to include transition-related goals as well as instructional goals. Fortunately, she had a few weeks for preparation, but she decided to spend some time right away reviewing the district's IEP manual. The manual stated that she needed to conduct a student interview, which she had planned to do anyway. Also, she needed to administer the Enderle-Severson Transition Rating Scale-J Revised (ESTR-J-Revised). The transition page of the district's IEP form requires that goals be written for these transition areas: instruction, employment, postsecondary education, social skills, and adult living. In the area of instruction, the goal is a

It All Depends

statement about remaining requirements for graduation with a standard or special diploma. For the other four areas, a student interview, parental concerns, and results of the ESTR-J-Revised are used for characterizing the student's present functioning level and identifying priority needs. When applicable, the statement "No needs in this area" is written.

She telephoned Isaac Reid to set up a time to pick up the ESTR-J-Revised. Later that day, she told him, she would be meeting with Nita, whose school was near the district office, and she hoped she could come by to see him before that meeting. Isaac explained that he would be out of the office all afternoon, but she was perfectly welcome to come. His office would be open, and his secretary would direct her to the forms, located in a file cabinet near his desk.

When Claire swung by the district office, Isaac Reid's secretary said she was expecting her and told her to take the needed materials. She found two rating scale forms, one for teachers and another for parents. She wasn't sure if the parent form was necessary. After all, they would be at the conference and could provide input if they desired to do so. If another goal or two were needed, they could be added. So she took only enough forms for each of Nita's teachers.

When Claire arrived at Nita's school, she proceeded to the library/media center where there was a small room that the librarian had offered her for the purpose of tutoring and meeting with students. When she entered, she saw Nita browsing the shelves of books. Nita, a delightful young lady, has always been an avid reader. She has a cochlear implant, which she received when she was four years old. She succeeded in developing functional speech and sign language skills. Her parents used Total Communication with her and gradually decreased signing as Nita continued to develop her auditory and oral skills. In school, however, she maintained her sign language skills as she communicated with the manual deaf students with whom she became acquainted.

Nita struggled in the general education classroom initially as she was simultaneously integrating the communication modalities available to her. A couple of years after cochlear implantation, with speech, language, and auditory intervention, she began to make

Case 23: A SMOOTH TRANSITION

significant academic progress. This favorable outcome is also attributable to her classroom teachers who have been remarkably diligent about optimizing the listening conditions in their classrooms as well as providing effective positional, visual, and instructional accommodations during lessons. Credit also is due her parents, who have consistently provided high levels of support over the years. Constant oversight of their daughter's education, as well as Nita's personal initiative and intelligence, has contributed to her successful inclusion into general education classrooms.

The approaching transition IEP conference was clearly a source of excitement for Nita, and she enthusiastically discussed her future and the milestones of emerging adulthood. She had received her driver's license, and her parents had purchased her a car, in which she could be seen driving all over town. She looked forward to voting next year when she turned 18, but said she had no idea about the process of registering. Her career aspiration came as no surprise. She wanted to become a librarian. She said she wasn't sure which colleges offered such a degree, but she definitely wanted to stay in the Southwest. She also said she wasn't exactly sure what librarians did and wondered aloud whether or not the librarian of the local library would allow her to volunteer over the summer. If so, that would be awesome, she said hopefully. Also, she had completed only half of the 20 service learning hours required for graduation, and the volunteer hours could count toward this criterion. This observation prompted Claire to ask about her progress toward the other two graduation criteria: passing the state proficiency examination and achieving 22 ½ credits with at least a 2.0 GPA in all required courses. Nita said she had taken and passed all sections of the statewide assessment. Also, she had accumulated 6½ credits of electives and 12½ credits of required courses. Therefore, during her senior year, she needed only 3½ credits in these courses: English language arts, mathematics, social studies, and computer literacy, which is a ½-credit course.

When asked what areas she felt she needed to work on to prepare herself for the future, she smiled and said she needed to learn more about finances. She has worked steadily as a babysitter for more than a year and admitted that she keeps her money in an envelope

It All Depends

under her mattress. Learning how to start a savings account would be useful, she said. This would help her avoid the temptation to spend her money so readily. Also, she learned in her social studies class that banks pay interest, and that would be nice. Money management would be especially beneficial when she goes to college, so starting now would give her some practice and experience.

Claire probed for other concerns. Nita closed her eyes, thought for a few seconds, and said that she needed to feel more comfortable and confident interacting with hearing students. To be happy in college, she said, she realizes that socialization will be necessary, not to mention its importance to her as a future librarian, a job that involves helping the public.

After having Nita complete a "Future Outcomes/Goals Assessment" sheet and finding out that her classes were going well, Claire thanked her for the productive discussion, adding that the information would be valuable in her upcoming IEP conference. When Nita left, Claire used the remainder of her workday to review the technical manual for the ESTR scales. She sent an e-mail message with the directions for completing the forms to each of Nita's teachers, also letting them know that she would place the forms in their campus mailboxes.

By the end of the following week, Claire had received the rating forms from all of Nita's teachers. They identified strengths in most areas but also indicated two possible areas of concern. The first was demonstrating necessary interpersonal skills to work with others. The second was practicing self-advocacy skills in a variety of settings. Also, in front of her, Claire had the notes she had written based on the interview she had conducted with Nita. Feeling overwhelmed for the moment, she quickly slipped all of the information into a folder. She felt pretty confident that, once she had some caffeine in her system, she would be able to translate the various needs and problem areas into goals consistent with the transition areas on the district's IEP form.

Ten minutes later, Claire had made a cup of coffee in the faculty workroom and returned to her work area. After a few sips, with less anxiety and more composure, she opened Nita's folder, determined to write some meaningful transition goals.

Case 23: A SMOOTH TRANSITION

QUESTIONS FOR REFLECTION

1. What are the key issues presented in this case?
2. How would you assess Claire's strengths and weaknesses as she prepares for the transition IEP conference?
3. What is a goal Claire could write in each of the transition areas listed below?
   - Instruction
   - Postsecondary education
   - Employment
   - Social skills
   - Adult living

EXTENSION ACTIVITIES

1. Identify commercially available materials designed to assess students' transition needs. These may include materials relative to social skills, life skills, work-related behavior, occupational interests, self-determination (including student-directed IEPs), employability skills, or any other domain of adulthood. For each resource, explain what areas are addressed and the specific population for which it is suitable.
2. Interview teachers of the deaf. Ask them how they incorporate transition skills into their lessons.
3. Gather several Individualized Transition Plan forms from various districts. Identify the ways in which they are similar and the ways in which they are different.
4. Identify Internet and print resources helpful to students, parents, and professionals in developing transition skills.

Case 24: Proposed Merger

Brynn Martel is having a blast teaching deaf fifth graders in a self-contained classroom, housed in a public school. Her students are not totally separate from their hearing peers, with whom they are enrolled in PE and art. Other interactions are exclusively social: on the buses, between classes, at lunchtime. During the first week of school, she and her students visited each of the other fifth-grade classes and taught their hearing peers basic signs that would facilitate interpersonal communication. Her students enjoyed sharing the language of signs, and the hearing students seemed to enjoy the experience of learning it.

It is Brynn's first year in the classroom, and she has just submitted quarterly grades for the very first time. Overall, her students performed well and, for the most part, she was pleased with her instruction. However, her positive reflection is tempered with a modicum of disquiet. Although her students grasp the academic content with apparent comprehension, she cannot disregard the fact that her students demonstrate some deficiencies with English language production. The problems did not mask the reality and quality of the students' content knowledge. Nonetheless, she felt that more needed to be done to increase their competence with the English language conventions expected of middle school students.

Brynn needed to share her uneasiness. In discussions with the other fifth-grade teachers, she did not feel that any of them genuinely appreciated her concerns. To date, she had avoided going to her superior. Because her students were learning grade-level content, she really did not feel she had a critical problem that needed external professional development. And she did not want to be viewed as a teacher who was inclined to bother district staff with every problem that arose. Nonetheless, she e-mailed Zander Witkin, the district's Supervisor of Hearing Support Programs and requested a meeting.

It All Depends

He explained that a late-afternoon meeting he was supposed to attend had been canceled, so he could meet with her later that day. She took him up on the offer.

After exchanging pleasantries and engaging in formulaic small talk, she proceeded to explain the issue that had been weighing heavily on her. Mr. Witkin listened attentively and patiently to her concerns. And rather than telling her to get a grip, which she had half-expected him to say, he did something that caught her totally off guard: He complimented her. First, he praised her for a successful first quarter. Second, he commended her foresight, agreeing that she had expressed a valid concern. Then, he pointed out that in the remaining 135 days of the school year, she could make a huge impact on her students' language abilities.

With great interest, Brynn leaned forward and said fervently, "Just give me some guidance. I'm willing to do anything to help my students improve."

He said, "I have obviously taken a look at the lesson plans you have written, since you have to submit those to your principal and to me. They are nicely done. However, on them, you identify only content objectives. And what's the result? Your students do well with the academic content. Right?"

Not wanting to appear boastful, she nodded and said hesitantly, "I would agree."

He continued, "I was recently watching a talk show, and the topic was effective parenting. The guest psychologist's suggestion to the beleaguered parents was that whatever they focused on grows. And that is my suggestion to you. Add language objectives to your content lesson plans, focus on those as well, and your students' content and language knowledge will grow. Actually, it is a concept that is the foundation of effective bilingual education practices, but it also has application in deaf education, I believe."

"Well, it certainly makes sense," she agreed. "But could you be more specific about how I can do this?"

"I certainly will," he replied. "The key is to look at your content and determine natural linkages to the English language arts standards in reading, language, and writing. For example, if you are teaching

Case 24: PROPOSED MERGER

about the 13 original colonies or significant individuals in the American Revolution, you could lay stress on the convention of capitalization because states and people are proper nouns. At the sentence level, let's say students are contrasting the properties of the inner and outer planets, a science benchmark, you could emphasize compound sentences with *but* to show differences between concepts, as well as appropriate transition words for compare/contrast writing."

"I think I get it," she said. "I will begin adding language objectives to my weekly plans, beginning next week. And I would love to get your feedback."

He smiled and said, "I would be very happy to provide it. I am sure you will do just fine. More important, I am confident you will see some changes in your students' written language production, which is the reason for our meeting. Good luck." He stood and extended his hand, which she reached out and shook appreciatively. She gave him a quick wave good-bye and left, feeling upbeat about the meeting.

As she was driving home, Brynn was mentally creating her to-do list: rake the leaves, clean the microwave, vacuum her car, and organize the bookshelves. Then her thoughts turned to the major science and social studies benchmarks she would begin teaching next week. Science: *Explain the parts of the water cycle.* Social Studies: *Identify important events in United States history.* She knew she would not be able to rest until she followed through on Mr. Witkin's suggestion. So there had to be an amendment to her plans. Determining language goals to complement these content benchmarks had just ascended to the top spot on her to-do list.

QUESTIONS FOR REFLECTION

1. What are the key issues presented in this case?
2. What are language arts concepts that might be infused into the two benchmarks presented in the case?
   - *Explain the parts of the water cycle.*
   - *Identify important events in United States history.*

It All Depends

3. Although the case focuses on science and social studies as the primary subjects into which language objectives are typically infused, math should not be overlooked for this purpose. What are two math topics that might provide opportunities for integrating language concepts?
4. Beyond planned academic lessons, what are two ways that teachers can cultivate additional opportunities throughout the school day to maximize deaf and hard of hearing students' reception and production of English?

Extension Activities

1. Locate the department of education site for a state in which you would like to teach. Identify six content standards (two for math, two for science, and two for social studies), and write language objectives that would complement each of the standards.
2. Students improve their writing by writing. To increase writing opportunities, many schools (K–16) have implemented writing across the curriculum (WAC) programs, which encourage writing in all subject areas. In WAC programs, there are two categories of writing: writing-to-learn (WTL) and writing in disciplines (WID). First, explain the difference between the two categories of writing. Second, identify three examples of writing formats that belong in each category.
3. A common approach for teaching hearing English language learners (ELLs) is specially designed academic instruction in English (SDAIE), which integrates language and content instruction. Summarize the overall approach, and identify five of its features that would also be useful when teaching deaf and hard of hearing students.

Case 25: From Finish to Start

Boyd Parker was tempted to pinch himself daily. He still could not believe that, two months ago, he had landed his dream job of teaching second graders in a bi-bi residential program. This job was the ideal combination of his desire to teach young children and to use the ASL skills he developed in college, thanks to a cadre of supportive deaf instructors.

Boyd's initial days in his teaching position had gone smoothly, in large measure because of the mentor he was provided to shepherd him during his period of induction. The Deaf Education Coordinator Violet Harris, with 20 years of teaching deaf and hard of hearing students at the elementary level and 5 years as a curriculum specialist, was an ongoing source of assistance and encouragement. Her professional background served as a treasure trove of proven strategies and promising practices. They met every two weeks and, prior to each meeting, she requested that he e-mail her a specific topic of concern, so that she could do whatever advance work was necessary to maximize their time together.

To date, Boyd felt comfortable with his instruction overall and, during interactions while teaching, his students' grasp of the standards was evident. Regrettably, however, there seemed to be a disconnect between the students' demonstration of knowledge during lessons and their demonstration of that same knowledge on summative assessments. Accordingly, in his most recent e-mail, he indicated that student assessment was problematic, and he summarized his concerns.

On the day of the meeting with Ms. Harris, she showed up promptly in his classroom at the appointed time. However, Boyd thought there must have been some miscommunication regarding the meeting's purpose when she began by saying, "Greetings. So let's get started with our discussion on lesson planning, as you requested."

It All Depends

Boyd evinced a puzzled expression and hesitantly said, "What I really wanted to discuss was assessment, to make sure I effectively evaluate students' understanding of the state standards."

With a genial smile, she said, "I suspected that would be your reaction. Actually, I approached the topic that way to suggest that assessment and planning are inextricably linked. Beginning teachers often think of assessment as what happens *after* learning experiences have taken place. I'm suggesting that you consider assessment *before* you consider all of those creative lessons you like to plan. Ever heard of Backward Design?"

"No," he responded, "but it sounds intriguing."

Ms. Harris unsnapped a brown leather portfolio, extracted a sheet of paper, and handed it to Boyd. As he perused it, she said, "Conceptually, it's similar to the second habit in Steven Covey's book *The 7 Habits of Highly Effective People*: Begin with the end in mind. This handout explains Backward Design in detail. But, in a nutshell, it is a planning process in which teachers actually identify the assessment evidence they will require of students before considering the instructional procedures. The reverse sequence is more typical—hence, the term Backward Design."

"What are the benefits of this approach?" Boyd asked, still fuzzy about this planning process.

She responded, "The main benefit is that if you begin with the assessment in mind, your instructional procedures can be more sharply attuned to enabling students to perform successfully when they are evaluated. Does that make sense?"

"Can you give me a specific example?" he inquired, still not totally clear about the process or its benefits.

"Sure," she said. "For example, let's say you plan to teach the Common Core literature standard 2.5, which states that second graders will describe the overall structure of a story. You determine that an appropriate assessment would be a completed story map."

"OK," he said. "So the assessment has been established."

She continued, "Because the assessment has been decided, your instruction would have a specific focus. First, you could show students an image of a story map. Second, you could explain the

Case 25: FROM FINISH TO START

components: characters, setting, problem, events, and resolution. Third, you could use a familiar story and complete a story map for it as you do a think-aloud. Finally, you could select another familiar story and complete a story map collaboratively with the students."

Nodding vigorously, Boyd said, "I see where this is going. Then, when I give the students a new narrative to read, the likelihood that they will be able to successfully complete a story map on their own is very high."

All at once, Ms. Harris stood and softly clapped her hands in Boyd's direction. "You're a quick study," she said. "My work here is done. While Backward Design might sound like an unusual approach to planning, many of the best teachers have always used it. Plus, it is in line with a standards-based approach to teaching, because the first step is identifying the standard. Anyway, try it for a couple of weeks, and the next time we meet, you can provide me with a status report. And if you require more detail, there is a great deal of information about Backward Design online."

"Thanks so much," he said enthusiastically. "I'm getting ready to write a social studies unit, and I can't wait to try Backward Design."

She said confidently, "I know you are equal to the task." Now that he had a coherent plan of action, he thought so, too.

After Ms. Harris left, Boyd decided to take a look at the next benchmarks he planned to teach in the four social studies strands in the state curriculum and consider appropriate assessments and engaging lessons for his students.

- *Identify the roles of the President, a governor, and a mayor.* (civics)
- *Explain the significance of national celebrations such as Independence Day and Memorial Day.* (American history)
- *Identify the basic elements of a physical map.* (geography)
- *Explain how work provides income to purchase goods and services.* (economics)

It All Depends

QUESTIONS FOR REFLECTION

1. What are the key issues presented in this case?
2. What are reasons that a discrepancy might exist between the knowledge acquisition of young deaf students and their test performance at the conclusion of a lesson or unit?
3. For each of the four social studies benchmarks at the end of the case, identify an assessment that would be appropriate for Boyd's second graders.
4. Choose one of the assessments from the previous question, and identify a set of lesson procedures that would teach the relevant information and lead to success on the assessment.

EXTENSION ACTIVITIES

1. Backward Design is only one instructional design model. Locate two other instructional design models, and summarize what they entail.
2. Although traditional assessments will, undoubtedly, always occupy a prominent role in American classrooms, many educators have come to recognize that alternative assessments can be powerful procedures for evaluating students' learning outcomes. Identify three specific examples of assessment strategies in each of these categories: nonverbal, products, and performances or presentations.
3. In addition to classroom assessments, district-wide and statewide tests are significant tools intended to measure students' achievement. IDEA mandates that appropriate accommodations be provided for students with disabilities, as necessary, to allow them to better demonstrate their knowledge and skills. Access your state's department of education assessment site, and identify accommodations allowed on these high-stakes tests for students with disabilities in general, as well as any accommodations intended specifically for students who are deaf and hard of hearing.

APPENDIX

Sample Rubrics for Assessing Students' Responses to Cases

On the pages that follow, two rubrics are included that instructors can consider for evaluating their students' responses to the questions for reflection that conclude each case study. They may be used as they appear, used with modifications, or disregarded entirely if instructors have other scoring guides or evaluation methods in mind that better suit the purposes of their courses.

The first rubric is *holistic* in nature and can be used to evaluate the totality of each response, focusing on its overall quality. The example provided is for Case 1, which has six questions. Instructors will need to simply adjust the rubric based on the number of questions asked in a particular case.

The second rubric is *analytic* and is intended to evaluate specific criteria representing the intellectual standards applied to the thinking processes in which students are expected to engage as they consider responses to the questions pertaining to each case.

It All Depends

Student Name _____   Case Study: "Listen Up"

Case Study Analysis Rubric: Holistic
Questions for Reflection

CRITERIA	NEEDS IMPROVEMENT	SATISFACTORY	EXCELLENT
Response to Question #1	1 2	3 4	5 6
Response to Question #2	1 2	3 4	5 6
Response to Question #3	1 2	3 4	5 6
Response to Question #4	1 2	3 4	5 6
Response to Question #5	1 2	3 4	5 6
Response to Question #6	1 2	3 4	5 6
Conventions of Written English	1 2 (8+ errors)	3 4 (4–7 errors)	5 6 (0–3 errors)
FINAL SCORE		_____ ÷ 42 x 100 = _____%	
Comments:			

APPENDIX

Student Name _____   Case Study: _____

Case Study Analysis Rubric: Analytic
Questions for Reflection

Grading Scale: 5 = Excellent 4 = Very Good 3 = Average 2 = Fair 1 = Poor					
Performance Criteria	5	4	3	2	1
Identification of Issues: Demonstrates a deep understanding of the main issues presented in the case study.					
Analysis of Issues: Provides a thorough, insightful analysis of the key issues presented in the case study.					
Recommended Solutions: Offers specific, realistic, and relevant suggestions consistent with the facts and concepts presented in the case study.					
Course Connections: Solutions are grounded in strong evidence and support based on concepts and principles derived from course readings, additional research, discussions with professionals in the field, or critical reasoning abilities.					
Writing Skills: Communicates ideas with clarity and precision, free of errors in writing conventions.					
TOTAL /25 = ____%					

Comments:

References & Related Readings

Allen, J. (2004). *Tools for teaching content literacy.* Portland, ME: Stenhouse Publishers.

Alvermann, D. E., Swafford, J., & Montero, M. K. (2004). *Content area literacy instruction for the elementary grades.* Boston: Pearson Education.

Arends, R. I. (2015). *Learning to teach* (10th ed.). Boston: McGraw-Hill.

Ashlock, R. B. (1990). *Error patterns in computation.* Columbus, OH: Merrill Publishing Company.

Bean, T., Baldwin, S., & Readance, J. (2012). *Content-area literacy: Reading and teaching the 21st century adolescent.* Huntington Beach, CA: Shell Education.

Bos, C. S., & Vaughn, S. (2006). *Strategies for teaching students with learning and behavior problems.* Boston: Pearson Education.

Bullard, C., & Luckner, C. (2013). *The itinerant teacher's handbook* (2nd ed.). Hillsboro, OR: Butte Publications.

Candler, C. (2012). *Laura Candler's graphic organizers for reading: Teaching tools aligned with the Common Core.* Saint Johnsbury, VT: Compass.

Chapman, C., & King, R. (2003). *Differentiated instructional strategies for reading in the content areas.* Thousand Oaks, CA: Corwin Press.

Chapman, C., & King, R. (2005). *Differentiated assessment strategies: One tool doesn't fit all.* Thousand Oaks, CA: Corwin Press.

Churchill, L. R., Mulholland, R., & Capello, M. R. (2008). *A practical guide for special education professionals.* Upper Saddle River, NJ: Pearson Education.

Currie, P. S., & Wadlington, E. M. (2000). *The source for learning disabilities.* East Moline, IL: LinguiSystems.

Developing quality individual educational plans: A guide for instructional personnel and families. (2000). Tallahassee, FL: Florida Department of Education.

Dove, M. G., & Honigsfeld, A. (2013). *Common Core for the not-so-common learner.* Thousand Oaks, CA: Corwin Press.

Dudley-Marling, C., & Paugh, P. (2004). *A classroom teacher's guide to struggling readers.* Portsmouth, NH: Heinemann.

Dunlap, C. Z., & Weisman, E. M. (2006). *Helping English language learners succeed.* Huntington Beach, CA: Shell Education.

Echevarria, J., Vogt, M., Short, D. J. (2000). *Making content comprehensible for English language learners: The SIOP model.* Boston: Allyn & Bacon.

Ertmer, D. J. (2005). *The source for children with cochlear implants.* East Moline, IL: LinguiSystems.

Forsten, C., Grant, J., & Hollas, B. (2003). *Differentiating textbooks: Strategies to improve student comprehension and motivation.* Peterborough, NH: Crystal Springs Books.

Gibb, G. S., & Dyches, T. T. (2007). *Guide to writing quality individualized education programs* (2nd ed.). Boston: Pearson Education.

Gregory, F. H., & Chapman, C. (2002). *Differentiated instructional strategies: One size doesn't fit all.* Thousand Oaks, CA: Corwin Press.

Hall, B. J., Oyer, H. J., & Haas, W. H. (2001). *Speech, language, and hearing disorders: A guide for the teacher.* Boston: Allyn & Bacon.

Harwell, J. M. (1989). *Complete learning disabilities handbook.* West Nyack, NY: The Center for Applied Research in Education.

Hull, R. H. (2001). *Aural rehabilitation: Serving children and adults.* San Diego, CA: Singular.

Kauffman, J. M., & Landrum, T. J. (2009). *Cases in emotional and behavioral disorders of children and youth* (2nd ed.). Upper Saddle River, NJ: Pearson Education.

Leber, N. J. (2002). *Easy activities for building social skills.* New York: Scholastic.

REFERENCES & RELATED READINGS

Lewis, W. E., Walpole, S., & McKenna, M. C. (2014). *Cracking the Common Core: Choosing and using texts in grades 6–12.* New York: The Guilford Press.

Luckner, J. L. (2002). *Facilitating the transition of students who are deaf or hard of hearing.* Austin, TX: PRO-ED.

Lyle, M. (1998). *The LD teacher's IEP companion: Goals, strategies, and activities for LD students.* East Moline, IL: LinguiSystems.

McCarr, J. E. (2002). *Lessons in syntax.* Hillsboro, OR: Butte Publications.

McEwan, E. K. (2007). *40 ways to support struggling readers in content classrooms, grades 6–12.* Thousand Oaks, CA: Corwin Press.

McKeough, A., Lupart, J. L., & Marini, A. (1995). *Teaching for transfer: Fostering generalization in learning.* Mahwah, NJ: Lawrence Erlbaum Associates.

McLoughlin, J. A., & Lewis, R. B. (2005). *Assessing students with special needs.* Upper Saddle River, NJ: Pearson Education.

Morrow, L. M., Shanahan, T., & Wixson, K. K. (Eds.). (2013). *Teaching with the Common Core Standards for English language arts: PreK–2.* New York: The Guilford Press.

Morrow, L. M., Wixson, K. K., & Shanahan, T. (Eds.). (2013). *Teaching with the Common Core Standards for English language arts: Grades 3–5.* New York: The Guilford Press.

Nolet, V., & McLaughlin, M. J. (2005). *Accessing the general curriculum: Including students with disabilities in standards-based reform.* Thousand Oaks, CA: Corwin Press.

Pierangelo, R., & Crane, R. (1997). *Complete guide to special education transition services.* West Nyack, NY: Center for Applied Research in Education.

Ralabate, P. (2003). *Meeting the challenge: Special education tools that work for all kids.* Washington, DC: National Education Association.

Reiss, J. (2005). *ESOL strategies for teaching content: Facilitating instruction for English language learners.* Upper Saddle River, NJ: Pearson Education.

Robb, L. (2009). *Reading strategy lessons for science and social studies.* New York: Scholastic.

Rose, S., McAnally, P. L., & Quigley, S. P. (2004). *Language learning practices with deaf children.* Austin, TX: PRO-ED.

Schirmer, B. R. (2000). *Language and literacy development in children who are deaf.* Boston: Allyn & Bacon.

Schleper, D. R. (1992). *Prereading strategies.* Washington, DC: Gallaudet University.

Severson, S., Enderle, J., & Hoover, J. (2003). *Transition planning in the schools: Using the Enderle-Severson Transition Rating Scales.* Moorhead, MN: ESTR Publications.

Silver, R. G. (2003). *First graphic organizers: Reading.* New York: Scholastic.

Stephens, E. C., & Brown, J. E. (2000). *A handbook of content literacy strategies: 75 practical reading and writing ideas.* Norwood, MA: Christopher Gordon Publishers.

Tomlinson, C. A. (2001). *How to differentiate instruction in mixed-ability classrooms* (2nd ed.). Alexandria, VA: Association for Supervision and Curriculum Development.

Turnbull, R., Huerta, N., & Stowe, M. (2009). *The Individuals with Disabilities Education Act as amended in 2004.* Boston: Pearson Education.

Venn, J. J. (2004). *Assessing students with special needs.* Upper Saddle River, NJ: Pearson Education.

Westphal, L. E. (2007). *Differentiating instruction with menus: Language arts, grades 3–5.* Waco, TX: Prufrock Press.

Westphal, L. E. (2007). *Differentiating instruction with menus: Social studies, grades 3–5.* Waco, TX: Prufrock Press.

Yopp, R. H., & Yopp, H. K. (2010). *Literature-based reading activities* (5th ed.). Boston: Allyn & Bacon.

Glossary

ADA Americans with Disabilities Act, which prohibits discrimination against individuals with disabilities in the areas of employment, transportation, public accommodations, telecommunications, and governmental activities

American Sign Language (ASL) a language employing manual communication combined with facial expressions and body language, used by many North Americans who are deaf

assessment the process of collecting information about student learning and performance before instruction (diagnostic), during instruction (formative), and after instruction (summative)

backward design (BD) an approach to instructional planning that involves identifying lesson goals before choosing methods of teaching and types of assessments

behavioral intervention plan a set of strategies developed to address the function of a student's misconduct in an effort to improve it

benchmark a specific description of knowledge and skills that students must master in order to demonstrate achievement of a related educational standard

case study a narrative description of a teaching scenario involving questions to be answered, problems to be solved, or decisions to be made

choice board graphic organizer containing a menu of learning activity options from which students can select to demonstrate they have learned a concept

It All Depends

cognates two words that have a common origin and, therefore, have the same meaning and the same or similar spellings, such as *class* (English) and *clase* (Spanish)

Common Core State Standards (CCSS) a set of academic expectations in mathematics and English language arts (ELA) that detail the knowledge and skills students should master by the completion of each grade level

concept attainment an approach to concept teaching in which students determine the attributes of a concept through a structured inquiry process of comparing and contrasting

congenital deafness a hearing loss that is present at birth

content literacy strategies ability to use reading and writing for the purpose of acquiring new information in specific subject areas

curriculum the set of learning standards in the various subject areas for each grade level

data chart diagram that organizes large amounts of information to make it more manageable

Deaf Studies a program of study designed to promote an understanding of Deaf people as a cultural group, drawing from the areas of language, communication, history, culture, and literature

differentiation an instructional approach that provides students with multiple options for learning academic content based on their individual strengths, needs, and interests

dyscalculia learning disability involving a severe impairment of mathematical ability

ELA acronym for English language arts, referring to reading, writing, language, and speaking and listening

GLOSSARY

feedback loud whistling or squealing sound resulting from the leakage of sound in an electronic device such as a hearing aid

FM system assistive hearing device that enhances the use of hearing aids and cochlear implants

formative assessment an assessment procedure used by teachers during the learning process to determine the need to modify teaching methods and learning activities

general curriculum the set of performance standards in a state that has been adopted for students without disabilities

general education teacher a teacher who instructs primarily students without disabilities, in a regular classroom setting

high-context situations interactions in which a large part of the information is conveyed through visual supports, facial expressions, and body language

IDEA acronym for the Individuals with Disabilities Education Act, a law enacted in 1975 to ensure that students with disabilities receive special education and related services to enhance their opportunities for school success

IEP acronym for Individualized Education Program, referring to a plan specifying educational goals for students with disabilities

instruction the process of implementing teaching methods designed to enable students to acquire knowledge and skills aligned with lesson objectives

intellectual disability a disability (once referred to as *mental retardation*) characterized by limitations in mental functioning and daily living skills

It All Depends

itinerant teacher   a teacher who travels to various schools and provides instruction to students with disabilities or consults with general education teachers who have students with disabilities mainstreamed into their classes

literacy coach   a school specialist who provides ongoing training and support for teachers to increase their effectiveness in improving students' reading and writing skills

literacy skills   the totality of skills needed for reading and writing, such as print awareness, vocabulary, spelling, and comprehension

manipulatives   objects designed to help students understand mathematical concepts through a hands-on approach

mentor texts   published pieces of writing used as examples to teach specific writing strategies or skills

multidisciplinary team   educators, specialists, administrators, and parents who determine needs-based goals for students with disabilities and identify services that support the achievement of these goals

multiple intelligences   a theory that intelligence is not a single general ability, and that people have a combination of strengths in a variety of specific areas

NCSS (National Council for the Social Studies)   an organization providing instructional support that enables social studies teachers to promote civic competence in their students

NCTM (National Council of Teachers of Mathematics)   an organization that provides guidance and resources for implementing research-based mathematics curriculum, instruction, and assessment

NSTA (National Science Teachers Association)   an organization devoted to promoting excellence and innovation in science teaching and learning

GLOSSARY

prereading strategies activities designed to help students activate prior knowledge, make connections, and formulate a purpose for reading

prewriting strategies activities designed to help students generate and organize ideas before drafting a writing assignment

resource room educational setting in which students with a disability are pulled from the regular classroom for a period of time to receive individualized and small-group instruction in areas requiring intensive academic support

SDAIE an acronym for "specifically designed academic instruction in English," an instructional approach for teaching academic subjects to students who have limited English proficiency by providing lessons that contain both content and language goals

self-advocacy an individual's ability to participate knowledgeably in making decisions about his or her life

self-contained classroom educational setting in which students with the same disability, similar achievement levels, and common learning characteristics are grouped together

self-determination the belief by individuals that they can control their own destiny by setting goals and working to achieve them

simultaneous communication a form of communication in which signs and speech are used at the same time

Six Traits a systematic approach to improving written language skills based on writing criteria that address ideas, voice, organization, word choice, sentence fluency, and conventions

state standards learning goals that describe what students are expected to know or be able to do at each grade level

It All Depends

strategy   a plan or method for achieving a desired goal or result

summative assessment   an assessment administered to students at the end of an instructional period (lesson, chapter, unit, quarter, semester, academic year)

task analysis   a process for breaking down more complex learning goals into specific subskills so they can be taught and mastered individually

text structure   the way that authors organize and present their ideas in reading material

transition   planning efforts intended to prepare secondary students to move from the world of school to the world of adulthood

transition goals   learning outcomes that target postschool outcomes such as employment, continuing education, and independent living

transition IEP   a document that specifies goals and services intended to prepare youth with disabilities for postsecondary educational opportunities, successful employment, and the responsibilities of community living

T-Unit   a measure of syntactic complexity that refers to a main clause plus all of the dependent clauses attached to it

Type-Token Ratio (TTR)   a measure of vocabulary development calculated by dividing the number of different words in a language sample by the total number of words in the sample